Tarot Reading Sta...

Your Tarot deck can answer not only the simple questions you many ask a fortuneteller, but also the deeper questions that ultimately direct your life. And if you begin an intense study of the Tarot for the purpose of personal spiritual development, you will eventually develop your own interpretations of the visual images on the cards.

But you need to start somewhere. You need to know the basic meanings of the cards before the Tarot can really "speak" to you in your own language. That's how *Tarot for Beginners* can help—by clearly describing and interpreting the symbolism of each of the 22 Major Arcana cards and the 56 Minor Arcana cards, and by showing you how to lay out the cards and interpret them in relation to each other.

The final judge of the true meaning of the Tarot is you. The Tarot is a key—and where there's a key, there's a door. Somewhere on the other side of this particular door, you will find the answers to all of your questions, whether simple or complex, secular or religious, spiritual or mundane. Let P. Scott Hollander—a student, teacher and reader of the Tarot for more than 20 years—show you what doors the Tarot can open for you.

About the Author

P. Scott Hollander has studied and used the Tarot for more than 20 years. Over the years, she has done more readings than she can count, both face to face and at long distance. She has also used the cards for counseling and some magical operations and has taught their use as meditation tools. (She feels she has reached the level of The Star in her own studies.) A professional freelance writer, she has been writing and publishing books, articles, and short stores for more than 25 years. She has been writing full-time since 1989. Her non-fiction texts and articles primarily cover arcane subjects, including a 1991 Llewellyn release, *Reading Between the Lines: The Basics of Handwriting Analysis*.

To Write the Author

If you wish to contact the author or would like more information about this book, please write in care of Llewellyn Worldwide, and we will forward your request. Both the author and publisher appreciate hearing from you and learning of your enjoyment of this book and how it helped you. Llewellyn Worldwide cannot guarantee that every letter to the author will be answered, but all will be forwarded. Please write to:

P. Scott Hollander
c/o Llewellyn Worldwide
P.O. Box 64383-K363, St. Paul, MN 55164-0383
Please enclose a self-addressed, stamped envelope for reply, or $1.00 to cover costs and an international postal reply coupon if necessary.

Free Catalog from Llewellyn Worldwide

For more than 90 years Llewellyn has brought its readers knowledge in the fields of metaphysics and human potential. Learn about the newest books in spiritual guidance, natural healing, astrology occult philosophy and more. Enjoy book reviews, new age articles, a calendar of events, plus current advertised products and services. To get your free copy of the Llewellyn's New Worlds of Mind and Spirit magazine, send you name and address to:

Llewellyn's New Worlds of Mind and Spirit
P.O. Box 64383-K363, St. Paul, MN 55164-0383, U.S.A.

Tarot for Beginners

*An Easy Guide to Understanding
& Interpreting the Tarot*

P. Scott Hollander

1995
Llewellyn Publications
St. Paul, Minnesota 55164-0383

FIRST EDITION
Third Printing 1995

Cover design by Anne Marie Garrison
Cover cards (from left to right) *Rider-Waite Tarot, Legend: The Arthurian Tarot, The New Golden Dawn Ritual Tarot*
Interior design and editing by Laura Gudbaur
Section page illustration by Anne Marie Garrison
Rider-Waite Tarot card illustrations reproduced from the designs by Pamela Colman Smith in the 1922 reprint of the original 1910 edition of *The Pictorial Key to the Tarot* by Arthur Edward Waite, William Rider & Son Ltd., London.
Other decks included: *Witches Tarot* by Ellen Cannon Reed and Martin Cannon, *The New Golden Dawn Ritual Tarot Deck* by Sandra Tabatha Cicero, *The Tarot of the Orishas* by Zolrak and Dürkön, *Legend: The Arthurian Tarot* by Anna Marie Ferguson, *The Healing Earth Tarot* by Jyoti and David McKie, all published by Llewellyn Publications.

Cataloging-in-Publication Data
Hollander, P. Scott
Tarot for beginners: an easy guide to understanding &
    interpreting the tarot/ by P. Scott Hollander. -- 1st ed.
    p. cm.
    ISBN 1-56718-363-8
    1. Tarot. 2. Fortune telling by cards. 3. Divination. I. Title
BF1879.T2H63   1995
133.3'2424--dc20   94-43321
                                                                CIP

Llewellyn Publications
A Division of Llewellyn Worldwide, Ltd.
P.O. Box 64383, St. Paul, MN 55164-0383

A prisoner devoid of books, had he a Tarot of which he knew how to make use, might in a few years possess a universal science, and discourse on all possible subjects with an unequalled doctrine and inexhaustible eloquence.

—Eliphas Levi

Dedication

For, my mom, Florence Hollander, who helped me look
inside my soul and find my own path.

Table of Contents

❀❀ **PART TWO:** The Minor Arcana ❀❀

❀❀ **PART THREE:** Divining with the Tarot ❀❀

Introduction

BEFORE YOU BEGIN

If you're like most people who have just begun a study of the Tarot (pronounced Ta-row), what you find most confusing is that there are so many different deck styles, and so many different interpretations of the cards. Where do you start? Whose interpretation is the one you should use?

It's not as complicated as it looks. The basic meanings of each of the cards are fairly standard. The reason different systems vary so much is because nearly everyone who uses a Tarot deck eventually develops their own interpretations of the imagery and symbolism shown on the cards.

As you will find, once you've chosen your own deck and a system you find compatible, the Tarot "speaks" to you. What's more, it speaks to you in your own language. Tarot imagery translates itself for you into whatever philosophical or religious viewpoint you need in order to understand and use your deck.

How different your personal interpretations will be depends on what you use your deck for. If you only want to use the Tarot to read fortunes, then all you need do is find an already existing system that makes sense to you (and gives you intelligible answers), and follow it. But the Tarot, especially the Major Arcana, can also be used as a path to your personal spiritual development. And if you begin an intense study of the Tarot for that purpose, you will eventually develop your own interpretations of the visual images on the cards.

What I'm going to do in this book is help you get started. I'll describe each of the cards in a standard Tarot deck, and give you its basic meaning. I will show you not only how to use your deck as a fortune-telling tool, but also how to begin to use it as a path to spiritual enlightenment.

Where you go from there is up to you. But you will find, if you do begin a serious study of the Tarot, that your deck can answer not only the simple questions you ask a fortuneteller, but also the real questions that ultimately direct your life.

The Tarot Deck

There are 78 cards in a Tarot deck, divided into the Major Arcana and the Minor Arcana. The word "Arcana" (singular: Arcanum) comes from the Latin *arcanus,* meaning closed or secret. In the context of the Tarot, it means a secret or a mystery, and is usually used in the plural form.

The Major Arcana, or trump suit, consists of twenty-two cards. Each card has a different picture which illustrates an action, behavior and/or event.

Each card also has a label, which is a name, a title, or a description of the picture on the card.

All the cards in the Major Arcana except one are numbered, from One to Twenty-One. The Fool, which is the only unnumbered card, is generally considered to be number Zero.

In a reading, the Major Arcana represents *states of being*—your mental, emotional, and/or spiritual condition at the time of the reading, or in terms of the situation being described.

The remaining fifty-six cards in your deck are called the Minor Arcana. These are divided into four suits: Swords, Cups, Coins, and Wands. There are fourteen cards in each suit: ten numbered (or pip) cards, from Ace to Ten, and four face (or court) cards: Page, Knight, Queen, and King.

In the reading, the Minor Arcana describes *events or situations,* and each suit focuses on a different area of your life. In general, Swords describe your mental or intellectual state, and Cups your emotional life. Coins correspond to your physical or material status, and Wands to career, abilities, or potentials. The court cards sometimes represent actual people in your life, or they may have the same kind of interpretation as the pip cards.

It is the cards of the Minor Arcana which correspond to today's modern deck of playing cards. In the modern deck, the Knight was eliminated, and the Page became the Jack, leaving only three court cards to each suit. The Tarot's Swords have become Spades; Cups became Hearts; Coins are called Diamonds; and Wands are Clubs. The only card from the Major Arcana that has made the transition from the Tarot to the playing deck is The Fool, which has become The Joker.

History of the Tarot

There are many theories about the origin of the Tarot, but no one knows for certain where and how the cards were first developed. Some authorities claim the Tarot evolved from the yarrow sticks used with the Chinese divination system called *I Ching*; others say that it was adapted from the legendary *Book of Thoth*. Still others place its origin as recently as fourteenth or fifteenth century Europe, since the earliest known complete deck dates from that time.

The most popular theory is that the Tarot was invented in ancient Egypt, and brought to Europe around the fourteenth century by wandering tribes of Gypsies. According to these scholars, the allegorical illustrations shown on the cards of the Major Arcana were derived from the teachings of the secret schools of Egypt.

Papus, in *Key to Occult Science*, explains that the kingdom was in danger of being overthrown, so the priests of ancient Egypt designed the Tarot as one way of preserving their secrets for initiates of future ages. The Major Arcana portrayed the stages of personal development required of initiates as they progressed toward the status of adept. By recording their teachings in a symbolic manner, it would be available to serious students of the occult arts, yet the Tarot deck itself would appear to be only an amusing game to the uninitiated.

Other schools of thought also theorize that the Major Arcana is a record of the secret teachings of various underground religious groups. One such group to whom the origin of the Tarot is attributed is the Gnostics, early Christian sects often considered heretical for their spiritual beliefs, who were indeed forced to take their faith underground to escape persecution.

Another theory suggests that the Tarot philosophy was derived from that of the Cabala. The order of the Major Arcana is indeed based on the Hebrew system of letters and numbers.

The Cabala is a mystical Jewish tradition which teaches that it is possible, through symbolic interpretation of ancient texts, to raise your consciousness above the level of mundane knowledge and lead you to an understanding of and union with the Divine. In this teaching, letters and numbers are not merely a way of writing down thoughts and events, but rather reservoirs of divine power which contain volumes of information and enlightenment accessible to the adept. (It is interesting to note that the Greek neo-Pythagorean school also taught that letters and numbers were divine beings which possessed their own supernatural powers.)

Many of the teachings of the Cabalists were never written down; they were passed from teacher to student by word of mouth and kept secret from outsiders. The kind of symbolism used in the Major Arcana is a way of preserving those secrets without making them readily available to the uninitiated. In this theory, then, the Tarot is an allegorical representation of the path to enlightenment, which again would be understandable only to those who were trained in this symbolic method of study.

The origin of the Minor Arcana is also in question. Some researchers believe they were part of the original Egyptian deck; others say they were added around the fourteenth century from an Italian card game known as *tarocchi*.

In fact, even the origin of the name "Tarot" is in doubt. One simple explanation is that the name was derived from the crossed lines which appear on the back of the cards, a design called *tarotee*. Others say the name comes from the *tarrochi*, which supplied the cards of the Minor Arcana.

Etteilla, a great exponent of the Tarot, explains that the name derives from the Egyptian words *tar*, "a path," and *ro* or *ros*, "royal," meaning together "the royal path of life." J.F. Vaillent (in *Les Romes, histoire vraie des vraise Bohemiens*, 1857), states that "the great divinity Ashtaroth, As-Taroth, is no other than the Indo-Tarter Tan-tara, the Tarot, the Zodiac." And still other authorities teach that both the Tarot and the Book of Thoth derive their names from the Egyptian word *taru*, meaning "to require an answer" or "to consult."

Whatever the origin of the Tarot, it is clear that the symbolism on the cards is universal, speaking to many different cultures and philosophies. People of all religious, ethnic, or national backgrounds have used the Tarot, and developed their own versions of the deck. And the one point on which all authorities agree is that the Tarot, especially the Major Arcana, contains a complete book of occult knowledge which can lead dedicated students to an understanding of both themselves and the mysteries of creation—if only you can learn to decipher their true meaning.

Using the Tarot for Divination and Meditation

In the last section of this text, I'll show you several ways to lay out your cards for fortune-telling with a Tarot deck, and how to make sense of the readings you get. At this point, however, it's important to understand how the Tarot works to find answers to your questions.

Though you may not believe it, you do have the innate ability to find the answers you need. But most of us can't access that ability on command. You use the Tarot—or any divination tool—as a way to focus your clairvoyance: to make it work when you want it to, and to make it help you find the truth on demand.

Think of your conscious mind as a kind of back-seat driver, the sort of busybody who always has all the answers—even when it doesn't know what it's talking about. In this case, of course, your back-seat driver is someone upon whose advice you usually do depend, which only makes it harder to ignore its unhelpful instructions.

Now you are driving on an unfamiliar road toward a place neither you, nor your backseat driver has ever been before.

You know that if you could just concentrate—on the road signs, on the positions of the sun and stars, on your own inner sense of direction—you could reach your destination with a minimum of trouble.

You're not allowed to concentrate, however. Every time you almost know which way to go, your back-seat driver chimes in with advice and instructions that throw you off.

The only way to effectively silence that back-seat driver is to give it something else to do; something that

will make your know-it-all (who actually knows nothing useful in this case) feel useful—which is actually all
it wants! That way, it will stop distracting you so you
can get to where you're going.

You can't simply ignore these unwanted instructions, because your back-seat driver needs to be
included; in fact, it cannot stop interfering even if you
both want it to. So the best thing to do is hand your
back-seat driver the road map and let it be the one to
read off the directions to you.

That's what any divination tool is for. It gives your
conscious mind something to do, so that your naturally
clairvoyant unconscious mind can concentrate on driving toward your destination.

Of all road maps to self-awareness and spiritual
development, the Tarot is the most detailed, yet most
concise, available.

In the chapters that follow, I'll give you the basic
meanings of the cards in both Arcana. As I said when
we began, how you actually wind up interpreting these
cards, once you begin serious readings, will be up to
you. The longer you work with the Tarot, the more personal your interpretation of each card will become.

Let it happen. Let the cards speak to you. If a particular reading "feels like" it means something other
than what any book on Tarot suggests it should mean,
go with your feeling. The Tarot is designed to draw on
your own clairvoyant subconscious to help you understand the truth.

The Major Arcana

Trumps

INTRODUCTION TO THE MAJOR ARCANA

The Major Arcana, also called the trump suit, is the heart of the Tarot. It is here, in these twenty-two picture cards, that the primary teachings of the Tarot are expressed. Whatever philosophy a given interpreter of the Tarot may follow will influence the design of these cards; further, that philosophy will also influence their interpretation of the Minor Arcana.

Each of the illustrations of the Major Arcana is an allegorical representation of a different state of being, or stage of spiritual development. Taken as a unit, the cards show the progression from neophyte, to initiate, to adept, in the mysteries the Tarot teaches.

There is no question but that the meanings of each of these illustrations are in fact both mystical and complex. But it is not necessary to discourage new students of the Tarot by using high-flown language to describe them. The basic meanings of the cards can be explained in simple English.

What I will do here is tell you the story each card illustrates, and give you a "starter's guide" to investigating the deeper philosophical implications of the cards for yourself. This way, whether you want to use the Tarot only for divination, or go on from there to explore its mystical meanings, you've got a point of departure for both.

How to Use This Guide

There are two ways you can use this text. If you want to use your deck only for fortune-telling, then in each chapter that follows skip to the section titled "In the Reading" and start there. If you want to use this book to begin a serious study of the Major Arcana, follow the procedure outlined below, then read each chapter in full.

In the first part of this text, each of the cards of the Major Arcana is described according to the same system. First you'll be given the name of the card and its correspondence: that is, both the number and the letter of the Hebrew alphabet with which it is associated.

Next is a statement of what the card represents: a brief explanation of the state of being, or stage of spiritual development, that the picture on the card is meant to illustrate.

Note that this is a very simplistic explanation of the meaning of the card. It is intended only as a jumping-off point for beginning your own investigation of the card's true meaning. If you're using the Tarot for fortune-telling, however, you can use this statement as a general guide to your querent's state of mind or personal characteristics in the situation the reading describes.

The next two sections of each chapter are intended to help you get started on uncovering the deeper meanings of the Major Arcana for yourself.

First there is a description of the illustration on each card. It covers the basic elements that you should notice and, where necessary, the underlying meaning of those elements.

Note here that illustrations on all decks differ to some degree. Some of these are superficial differences; in costume, in the gender of the figures, and so forth. Some of them are elements which have been added to the illustration to complement or reinforce the basic philosophy of the designer of any given deck.

But there are elements in the illustrations of the Major Arcana which are the same—or should be the same—in all decks. Those are the elements which are described in these chapters. The "Description" section assumes that you're working with only one deck and therefore have no way to compare decks and see what they have in common. So the primary purpose of this section is simply to tell you which elements on each card are so vital to the basic meaning of the Tarot that they are repeated in all decks.

The second part of the meditation section, "Meaning," explains the allegory the card represents. Here again, an attempt has been made to eliminate any interpretations that are specific to a given religious or philosophical system, and just give you the basic, or standard, interpretation of the cards.

As before, this description is just a starting point. What you get from each card, in the end, should be your own.

How to Begin Your Own Interpretation

Before you even read these chapters, examine each Major Arcana card in your own deck carefully. Notice the main figures on the card, their positions (seated or standing, relationships to each other, how they hold their hands or position their bodies, etc.), any figures, human or otherwise, that accompany them, any props or tools they may have, any points about the background that stand out in your mind.

Note that every detail on each card is a meaningful symbol, even something as minor as a clump of grass somewhere in the background, and that each card contains a number of elements which must be considered in interpreting its overall meaning. While there are elements of major importance (those which are, as mentioned above, present in all decks), individual decks add their own symbolism, and this creates a different slant or perspective in the interpretation of the card. Teach yourself to notice everything each illustration contains.

Keep in mind, as you study your cards, that many cultures have contributed to the Tarot. If there is anything in the philosophical symbolism of the illustrations that you find uncomfortable, you're working with the wrong deck. For example, there are decks that use obviously Christian symbology, others that are just as obviously Pagan, or Feminist, and so forth. If your religious, or even political, philosophy is in conflict with that of the designer of your deck, you will not be able to use that deck for meditation. You may not even be able to use it for simple fortunetelling.

There are also, unfortunately, some decks that use a confusion of symbology. (I've seen one in which a Pagan

High Priestess, wearing a crescent moon headdress, is followed by a Roman Catholic Pope holding a triple cross). I would suggest that you avoid this type of deck as well. Find a deck that is consistent in its own symbology, and that complements your own basic philosophy.

Once you have studied each illustration, write down your impressions of the card: details of the illustrations, what each detail means to you, what you think the card as a unit has to say. The Major Arcana is a book of disguised knowledge. Try to decide for yourself what it is each illustration is trying to tell you.

It may seem like a waste of time to begin your study unaided when you have a learner's guide available, but it is very important for you to make this first examination on your own. This is an opportunity you will get only once: because once you've read someone else's impression of the Tarot, that will forever affect how you see the cards.

After you've looked over each card and noted down your own impressions, then read the descriptions in these chapters. See if you identified at least some of the important elements of each card. You'll probably find that you did.

You'll also probably find that your first impressions of what these elements mean will differ from the explanations you find here, or in any other text. It doesn't mean that your interpretation is wrong. *There are as many interpretations of the cards of the Major Arcana as there are readers.* If your first impression of each card varies from someone else's, it means that the illustration has reached something in your own unconscious, in your own personal experiences, that is unique to you. What you derive from your own untutored examination of these cards will be an extremely significant factor in your later study of the Tarot.

Don't question it, or even try to understand it at first. Just keep a record of it. If you do complete an intensive study of the Tarot, you may be surprised to find how meaningful your first intuitive impressions of the cards were when you read them over later.

If you don't get a significant impression from any of the cards—or even from just some of the cards—then once again, you're working with the wrong deck. Find one that does speak to you. It's out there somewhere.

Using Your Deck for Fortunetelling

The last section of each chapter is called "In the Reading." This tells you the meaning of the card as it applies to simple divination. The emphasis here is on fortunetelling, not meditation, so there's a slightly different viewpoint in the interpretations of the cards.

This section lists a number of statements describing both the positive and negative aspects of each card as it applies to a reading. The card does not mean all these things at once. When doing a reading, you pick the description which makes the most sense in the context of the question you're answering, and/or which relates best to surrounding cards. (See the chapter on divination for further explanation of this procedure.) There is also, for each card, a general description of the querent's mental or emotional state as shown by the presence of that card in a reading. This may be presented as a question or a statement or both. In explaining the reading, you can either choose an appropriate phrase from the list of positive or negative characteristics, or use this description as your guide to the meaning of the card.

Note that, in an ordinary reading, when a trump card comes up it describes how the querent feels, or is likely to react, in the situation being described. In effect, the trump card states: "This is the kind of person you are right now"—or, "This is the kind of person this situation has turned you into." Naturally, the kind of person you are right now is going to affect how you deal with any given situation. In a reading, therefore, trump cards are considered as a major influence on other cards, and on the situation as a whole.

A Note on the Order of the Cards

In a reading, trump cards may come up one at a time and in any order, and are considered merely in terms of their position in the layout, or spread, but in meditation, the cards of the Major Arcana cannot operate independently of each other. Each card leads to the next, and follows from the one before. Which means it is necessary to know their proper order.

Unfortunately, the experts cannot agree even on this. Some decks, for example, place The Fool at the beginning, others at the end, and still others as second to the last. (And as you will see when you get to that chapter, this not only changes its numerical correspondence, but also the possible underlying meaning of this card.)

In addition, at least two writers on the Tarot (A.E. Waite and Paul Case) switch the order of two other cards within the Major Arcana: Strength and Justice. They number these cards as eight and eleven, respectively, while almost every other Tarot deck shows them in exactly the opposite order.

My advice on this issue is simple: don't drive yourself nuts with the order. If you are only using your deck for divination, the order of the Major Arcana doesn't matter at all. The order of the cards will be important if you intend to use the Tarot as a spiritual guide, but if you do begin an intensive study of the Tarot, then as you gather more information, both as the result of reading this and other texts and using your deck for meditation, you'll eventually reach your own conclusions as to which order makes the most sense. If, in your study of the Major Arcana, it seems that one step should come before the other, then you can renumber your deck according to that system. But don't let these scholarly disagreements stop you from learning the cards in the first place.

What I've done here is list the cards in the order most decks use; any exceptions to that order are noted where they occur in other decks. Just take it from there.

The Tarot as a Spiritual Guide

Since the pictures on the Major Arcana are allegories, let's employ an allegory to explain how to use what they teach.

The Tarot is one of the paths to spiritual self-enlightenment. It teaches you not only how to reach this goal, but also warns you of the wrong turns you can take along the way.

It is easiest to understand the nature of your journey if you think of the Major Arcana as an ascending staircase with twenty-two steps. Each step has a slightly different configuration; some are wider, some narrower, some are rougher, some smoother. And each step has its own unique obstacles which you must overcome in order to make your way across it.

The passage between steps varies in difficulty as well. In some cases, you may have a steep and torturous climb; in others, passage may be as simple as stepping through a doorway. There is always a barrier, however, which you must figure out how to cross in order to make your way to the next stage upward.

Each step also has a landing, leading off the main staircase, where the climber can stop and rest—or get off the upward road forever—and here there are no barriers. What you see on these landings is sometimes terrifying, sometimes beautiful, sometimes both at once, bu it is always alluring. Each landing has its own temptations, drawing you toward it. And whatever you see on any landing, and however it affects you, it is always easier to step off onto the landing than it is to make your way across the step you're on, or upward to the next one.

You begin at the bottom of this staircase as a seeker trying to find answers to the basic human questions: Why am I here? What is life really supposed to be all about? Those who have made this climb before you can give you a general idea of what you will find on each step, what the temptations on each landing may be, and how difficult it is to proceed from one step to another, but no one can tell you exactly what you will find at any stage, or how you will react: each seeker is different.

All that you do know for certain is that there are twenty-two steps, and that you must climb them all to reach your goal. If you stop at any point less than twenty-two, you may find what you think you were really looking for. But you will never find the true answers to your questions.

Every path to spiritual self-enlightenment has its own dangers, and its own opportunities for failure, and the Path of the Tarot is no exception. There will be times when you despair, when you're certain you'll never understand or succeed, when you are tempted to quit.

But if you persevere, you will have one very important advantage working in your favor. You will find, at each step, that you already possess the qualities you need to win through. The Tarot does not give them to you: it doesn't need to. These qualities exist within you, and always have. The teachings of the Tarot are intended only to help you bring them out, so that you can use them to achieve your own best destiny.

These are the decks used in this book to illustrate the Tarot.

The Healing Earth Tarot, by David and Jyoti McKie, emphasizes Earth as a planet of healing through a variety of cultures' shamanistic images. It is characterized by its geometric border.

The New Golden Dawn Ritual Tarot, by Sandra Tabatha Cicero, follows the Western magickal tradition of the Golden Dawn. It is distinguished by its presentation of the corresponding Hebrew letter, planetary and zodiacal symbols.

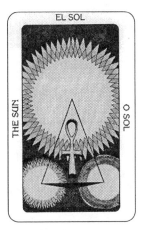

The *Tarot of the Orishas*, by Zolrak and Dürkön, is based on the African Candomblé religion. It is labeled in three languages, English, Spanish, and Portuguese

The Arthurian Legend Tarot, by Anna Marie Ferguson, is based in the old Grail and King Arthur legends. It is distinguished by its Celtic style and ornate border.

The Witches Tarot, by Ellen Cannon Reed, uses pagan and Qabalistic imagery in an exploration of the Tree of Life. It is characterized by having no border.

The traditional Rider-Waite deck, as drawn by Pamela Coleman Smith, is representative of medieval Tarot. It is characterised by its heavy black and white drawings

SHAMAN

The individual pictured in this card is someone with the ability to control and manipulate people, things, and events.

I

THE MAGICIAN

I THE MAGICIAN

Trumps One

THE MAGICIAN

Le Bateleur (The Juggler), usually called The Magician. Corresponding to the number One, also to the Hebrew letter Aleph.

Represents

Human intelligence; worldly wisdom. Control of (or, the need to control and manipulate) the forces that operate in this world.

Description

In most decks, the Magician is male; in all decks, this figure stands alone. Male or female, the Magician has a young face and wise eyes; he is ageless.

Costume varies, depending on the deck, from Egyptian to Greek to Medieval. The Magician always, however, wears a belt, and in some decks this belt is a coiled serpent (possibly Ourobouros, the alchemical serpent swallowing its own tail, or perhaps the serpent that both Moses and the Egyptian magicians were able to make come alive from their staffs).

The Magician stands with one hand raised, usually holding a wand, the other hand pointing downward. The down-pointing hand may or may not be holding some other object. (Note that this position mirrors the shape of the letter Aleph.) The symbolism here is "As Above, So Below." This is the teaching of Hermes Trismegistus that the smaller world within each person contains all the elements of the larger universe, and the study of a single individual—yourself—can lead to an understanding of all creation.

Spread out before the Magician, usually on a low table (or possibly an altar), are various objects. In some decks, these are just miscellaneous objects. In other decks, there are four distinct shapes which depict the four suits of the Minor Arcana: a cup, a sword, a wand, and a pentacle. Here, note that since the world represented as being under the control of the Magician is that of the Tarot, it makes sense that the objects be of the Minor Arcana. If other objects show in your deck, however, it is not necessarily incorrect.

In any case, the objects represent things which the adept has under his control. And that is the essence of this card: control of your Self and of the elements of your universe.

Meaning

Whether you think of this card as The Magician or The Juggler, the allegory is the same. Consider that everything in the universe is spread out before God like the objects on The Juggler's table, and these elements of creation are tossed about by God in the same manner that a juggler tosses his objects around. The objects themselves are not important to The Juggler as individuals. The ability to manipulate and control them is.

If you consider this card as The Magician, then in occult teachings, a true magician stands at the center of the universe, and all things radiate out from him. However he creates, or recreates, the nature of the universe within his mind becomes the nature of the universe in fact. So either way, the individual pictured in this card is someone with the ability to control and manipulate people, things, and events.

Tarot Arcanum One is the first step on the road to spiritual enlightenment and self-development. It's also the place where too many people stop. Because The Magician, or Juggler, does have control of his world, and control of others as well, it's tempting to consider this the goal you're seeking.

You begin on your path with Will—the decision to grow; the hope of success. In terms of a Magician, the question is, do you stay with control of the mundane world, or go on from there to grow spiritually? In terms of the Juggler, the question is: How many objects can you keep in the air at the same time, and for how long?

In the Reading

Upright (or Positive): Strength of will, intuition, self-control, self-confidence, autonomy, diplomacy. The positive qualities of humankind: skill, initiative, intelligence, discernment, and comprehension; freedom from control by others. All leading to success and the ability to control your environment.

Reversed (or Negative): Cleverness, lack of scruples, trickery, cunning, subtlety. An intriguer, a liar, a charlatan, a rogue; one willing to exploit the weaknesses and trust of others. All resulting from a lack of real self-esteem, and domination by outside forces; sometimes leading to disgrace or mental imbalance.

In effect, the Magician is one who has the potential to be like a god. If this card represents the querent, then you are one who has the power (or the potential for it) to control your immediate world. Are you developing this potential or throwing it away on demonstrations of mundane power? The rest of the cards in the reading will tell you.

THE HIGH PRIESTESS

This card represents the ability to understand and interpret the word of God—the understanding of the Law which is the highest and best use of our intellectual ability.

OCHUN

OSHUN

OXUM

THE HIGH PRIESTESS

THE HIGH PRIESTESS

Junon/La Papesse (The High Priestess, or High Popess)
Corresponding to the number Two; also to the Hebrew
letter Beth.

Represents

Divine wisdom; enlightenment. Understanding of (or
the need to understand) the reasons things work the
way they do.

Description

A female figure, either seated or standing. If standing,
she is holding a staff and pointing toward something in
the distance; if seated, in many decks she is holding an
open book, representing the divine law that rules and
orders the universe. Again, costume may vary, but

however she is dressed, she wears the Crescent crown (or some variation of it).

In most decks, the priestess stands or is seated between two pillars, or columns; usually, one pillar is black and the other is white. This theme repeats on other cards in the Major Arcana. You can consider the pillars to represent good and evil, light and darkness, truth and lies. The best place to start, however, is to look at them as the portals of a doorway, and the figure between them as the Guardian of that Gate. In order to pass through the gate, you do not have to defeat or placate the Guardian. You have to become whatever that Guardian is.

The High Priestess represents divine wisdom. She is at once Goddess, Mother, Protector, Teacher. Unlike The Magician, who uses his skills to manipulate the universe, The High Priestess exists to protect and teach rather than control. She is one who understands how the universe works, and it is that understanding, rather than simple control of these forces, which is both her goal and the essence of her being.

The essence of this card is wisdom—understanding of the laws that underlie the workings of the universe.

Meaning

If you opt for the right-hand path of spiritual growth, then The High Priestess is your next step. She understands the workings of the universe, the why of things. And she uses her understanding not to control and manipulate, but to nurture, teach, and protect.

This card represents the ability to understand and interpret the word of God; the understanding of the Law which is the highest and best use of our intellectual ability.

As a representation of Divine Law, The High Priestess is that Law incarnate, or as much of it as can be comprehended by mortal beings. She is the female creative force; the mother of all wisdom, the female aspect of God. She teaches that the knowledge and understanding you seek is within you; in your subconscious mind. To tap it, you must bypass your conscious mind, or avoid being deceived by your sensual and worldly nature.

Note, however, that while the goals of The High Priestess may be considered more worthy (and certainly less selfish) than those of The Magician, they are still not the place where the seeker should stop. The High Priestess is also one who expends her energy on nurturing and teaching others. That, too, limits her ability to grow spiritually in her own right.

In the Reading

Upright (or Positive): Wisdom, serenity, knowledge and understanding. Judgement, learning, mystery, science, art. The ability to learn and to teach. Also; possible secrets that will be revealed in their proper time.

Reversed (or Negative): Superficial knowledge, even ignorance; inability to judge events and issues clearly; muddy thinking; prejudice and one-sidedness. Also, a reluctance, or fear of making decisions.

The High Priestess is the one who knows the Way—and is willing to lead you there, if you're willing to go. If this card represents the querent, then you are one who is able to set others on the right road. But be careful. Don't be so concerned with their well-being that you neglect your own opportunities.

THE EMPRESS

THE EMPRESS.

III THE EMPRESS

The Empress is the matriarch incarnate, representing security, comfort (both physical and emotional), and understanding.

THE EMPRESS

L'Imperatrice (The Empress). Corresponding to the number Three, also to the Hebrew letter Gimel.

Represents

The Mother, procreation, and domestic harmony—not just in the individual home, but in society as a whole.

Description

Mature female figure seated on a throne, dressed in fine robes. She holds a scepter and is wearing an imperial crown. In some decks, a shield, or coat of arms, is at her feet, leaning against the foot of her throne. Also, in some decks, her throne is in a garden; in most decks she is outside. The Empress is a mother figure, with all that that implies: she is both a creative force and the one who insures that the different elements she brings into this world work together, not in opposition. The essence of this card is the harmonious cooperation of otherwise opposing forces, working together toward a common goal—domestic harmony and personal fulfillment for all concerned. The Empress is the matriarch incarnate, representing security, comfort (both physical and emotional), and understanding.

Meaning

The Empress is the female ruler of the house—the Mother. She understands how things have to work in this world in order for her subjects (whom she treats as her children) to be safe, happy, and content; she has the power to make certain things do work in harmony.

She is also the symbol of feminine instinct—intuitive flashes that enable you to make the right decision when there is no time for conscious thought. She is protection and fertility. She teaches love between people (the union of souls, as opposed to mere sexual attraction). As the Mother, she is the door or gate through which we enter this world; as a ruler, she insures harmony and the ability of people to work with each other, rather than at odds with each other. The Empress is the ruling force which creates an environment in which each person is free to develop their own individual potential.

In the Reading

Upright (or Positive): Fruitfulness of action, beauty, personal development and progress. Domestic harmony. Marriage, and maternity. Long life. Understanding derived from personal experience. Both emotional and physical comforts; she provides not only the necessities of life, but also luxuries.

Reversed (or Negative): The unknown. Doubts and difficulties. Indecision. Selfishness. Loss of power, inability to solve problems or make useful plans. Vacillation, ignorance.

The Empress is the one who knows how to make this world run smoothly, if you are willing to listen (to her) and cooperate (with others). If this card represents the querent, then you are one who can make things work smoothly and well for others—if you can make them listen and understand.

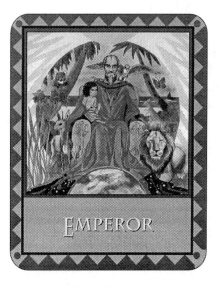

The Emperor represents a different kind of worldly wisdom: the understanding that it is not enough to want peace and security, or even to teach it; sometimes you have to be willing—and able— to defend it.

Trumps Four

THE EMPEROR

L'Empereur (The Emperor) Corresponding to the number Four, also to the Hebrew letter Daleth.

Represents

The Father. Worldly power, and protection of those for whom he is responsible.

Description

Mature male figure (usually with a full beard) either seated on or leaning against a throne. He wears his robes over a full suit of armor. He carries a scepter and wears an imperial crown. In some decks, a shield or coat of arms rests beside his throne or at his feet. Again, his throne is outdoors, sometimes with mountains in the distance. The essence of this card is protection—the willingness to fight for the domestic harmony that the

Empress teaches. The Emperor is the male protector of the home, the father who guards and guides all those within his care.

Meaning

The Emperor is also a wise teacher. In this case what he teaches is the meaning and use of worldly power. There are forces that no amount of good will or proper training can overcome: sometimes you have to be willing to pick up a sword. The Emperor teaches that you cannot compromise with your conscience; what is worth having must also be worth fighting for, if necessary. As the male protector of the home, The Emperor is ruler and patriarch, the defender of his world. The Emperor represents a different kind of worldly wisdom: the understanding that it is not enough to want peace and security, or even to teach it; sometimes you have to be willing—and able—to defend it.

In the Reading

Upright (or Positive): Authority, accomplishment, worldly power, stability, wisdom, ambition, reasoned action. Leadership, and ability to govern wisely. Compassion. Protection. Aid. Goals reached and won.

Reversed (or Negative): Immaturity and confusion. Loss of power. Problems with enemies. Inability to reach your goals; dissipation of energy.

As the Empress teaches people to work together, the Emperor guards this safe home against dangers from outside. If this card represents the querent, then you are one who is able to defend—and willing to die for—the people and things you treasure. Make certain that whatever you are defending is worth dying for.

MASTER

The High Priest in the Tarot specifically represents religious authority—the search for truth, the interpreter of secret mysteries, the one who points the way to salvation (or whatever your ultimate spiritual goal may be).

EL BABALOCHA

THE BABALORISHA

O BABALORIXÁ

5 THE HIEROPHANT

TALIESIN

Trumps Five

THE HIGH PRIEST

The Hierophant (The High Priest). In some decks Jupiter (or Zeus); in others, the Pope. Corresponding to the number Five, also to the Hebrew letter He.

Represents

Divine Will; interpretation of the Law of God in terms of personal and social codes of behavior.

Description

A male figure, seated on a throne. He is dressed in priestly vestments, crowned, and holding a scepter, usually in his left hand. The High Priest's accoutrements depend on which deck you are using. His scepter bears the representative symbol of whatever religion the deck's designer follows; his crown and

robes are also identifiable as part of the priestly vestments of that particular faith. The High Priest's free
hand is raised in blessing. Standing before him, or
seated at his feet, are two (in some decks three) lesser
priests, either paying him homage or in some way peti-
tioning him. In some decks, The High Priest has a very
young face, even somewhat effeminate; in others he is
old and bearded.

In almost all decks, this figure, like the High Priestess (Arcanum Two), is seated between two columns.

The essence of this card is religious authority. This
is the personage who has the power—given him by his
followers or believers—to decide what you must do to
be "saved."

Meaning

Whatever your supreme deity, it is evident that he or
she does not descend from the heavens at regular inter-
vals to speak directly to the general populace. So most,
if not all, religions have individuals whose task it is to
interpret the divine will for their followers. The more
organized or structured the religion, the greater the
authority of its High Priest.

The point to remember here is that it is not only in
organized religion that some human representative
possesses this kind of authority. The High Priest in the
Tarot specifically represents religious authority, the
search for truth, the interpreter of secret mysteries, the
one who points the way to salvation (or whatever your
ultimate spiritual goal may be).

But this figure also symbolizes any organized
philosophical or educational institution, be it religious
or temporal, that exerts that kind of mind control over

its followers. In all such institutionalized philosophies, there is someone, or some controlling group, who insists that they are the only ones who know the truth, and you either obey their word or are damned.

In Arcanum Five, you are being challenged to decide. At this particular stage of your spiritual development, you are given the opportunity to uncover the ultimate mystery—to discover the Will of God as it applies to you. Again, the High Priest is the Guardian of a Gate: to get through you must become him. Do you decide for yourself what is the road to your salvation, or do you let some other authority—even that of the Tarot!—think for you? What you decide now will affect the rest of your spiritual development from this point on.

Note that this is not always a favorable card. Unlike The High Priestess, who uses her wisdom and understanding to enable others to find their true path, The High Priest uses his power to increase his own authority over others. This card presents you with the choice of exploring your own soul's needs, or adapting your Self to the requirements of others.

In the Reading

Upright (or Positive): Mercy, goodness, kindness, alliance (including possible marriage). Creativity. The search for Truth. Understanding and inspiration. Religious needs and inclinations. Moral courage; the ability to go your own road if you believe it's right, despite opposition.

Reversed (or Negative): Extreme conservatism; over-kindness or over-conformity. Servitude, captivity, weakness. Need to be socially approved and accepted. The need to conform. Loss of personal authority (or, acceptance of authority only when there's someone to blame if things go wrong.)

This card represents someone who has the actual power to advance or defeat you. You must decide if the advancement you want is worth placating this individual. If this card represents the querent then you are someone who insists on deciding vital issues for others, usually in a way that enhances your own ability to continue to do this. You run the risk of surrendering real authority and personal growth to a belief in your own infallibility.

LOVERS

The Lovers allegory is of a union of opposites, pictured here as male and female, and of the mystical bond between those who are alike in spirit.

THE LOVERS.

VI THE LOVERS

Trumps Six

THE LOVERS

L'Amoureux (The Lovers). Corresponding to the number Six, also to the Hebrew letter Vav.

Represents

Union of opposites; commitment.

Description

Not counting supernatural figures (described below), some decks show only two young lovers, who may be either clothed or nude. Others show a third person either observing or in some way influencing the outcome of their match. In several medieval-style decks the third party is an older man; he may be either an observer, or a parental figure to whom the young couple are evidently explaining themselves. In Egyptian-style decks, the trio shows a young man and two young women between whom he obviously has to choose.

In decks which show three human figures, there is a winged cupid-style figure leaning out of a cloud above them, whose arrow points toward the woman (or one of the two young women). In decks that show only two young lovers, the supernatural influence above them is a winged angel with its hands outspread in blessing; the choices necessary for them to make are shown in other imagery (for example, Waite's deck depicts an Adam and Eve pair standing before the Tree of Knowledge and the Tree of Life, respectively)

The necessity of making a choice is as much a part of the allegory behind this card as is the union of two young lovers.

Meaning

The Lovers allegory is of a union of opposites, pictured here as male and female, and of the mystical bond between those who are alike in spirit. It can refer to romantic love, or an ideal friendship, or some other close bond between two people, especially when there has been some kind of barrier or opposition which the two souls involved must or will overcome in order to join. If this is the case, then it is mutual commitment that is the essential element which unites those whose lives must run together.

But there are other kinds of "marriage," and other kinds of opposites that need to be reconciled. As an allegory of your personal spiritual development, The Lovers depicts the union of opposites within yourself. Each of us has qualities which we perceive as positive or negative, and traits which are apparently in conflict. And for each of these qualities or traits, there are those which we accept and others which we would prefer to eliminate; some, in fact, which we don't even want to admit we have.

The Lovers asks you to explore and reconcile these opposites within yourself rather than attempting to eliminate or change them. By understanding and utilizing both sides of your own nature, you become a coherent whole, no longer in conflict with yourself. And because this is a difficult task, once again it is commitment which is required of you in order to reach your goals.

You are not simply being asked to accept the presence of these different traits. You are being asked to understand that even the ones you don't approve of are necessary to your continued growth and well-being. Opposite does not mean one is good and one is evil. The opposite traits within yourself—or within the other person with whom you are trying to bond—are mirrors of each other, which complement and can support each other. What needs to be accomplished here is a union of these opposites: a way of making them work together which eliminates their conflicts and creates a whole greater than the sum of its parts.

The reward for resolving the disparate elements within yourself is an increase in your own strength and will. You no longer waste time and energy struggling—uselessly!—to eliminate qualities in yourself or others that disturb you. Instead, you integrate them into yourself and then can use them to further your own control of situations and events.

In the Reading

Upright (or Positive): Attraction, love, problems or trials overcome by harmony, union, cooperation. Wise decisions: the correct choice made (perhaps between two equally worthy goals); a possible struggle, but with happiness as the outcome

Reversed (or Negative): Failure, conflict, division, immature planning, frustration. Unrealistic goals. Poor choices. Unhappiness.

As the High Priest card suggests that your best road is to develop your own will rather than accept the requirements of others, The Lovers reminds you that those others—either people or forces—have characteristics or elements that you need to survive and grow. If this card represents the querent, then you are about to be faced with an important choice that will influence the course of your life from now on. You must decide—hopefully wisely—what you are going to do. And whatever you choose, you must commit your energies to making it work if you expect to succeed.

The Chariot pictures mastery of real opposites, control over and use of those things which are by their nature in conflict.

THE CHARIOT

Le Chariot (The Chariot). Corresponding to the number Seven, also to the Hebrew letter Zayin.

Represents

Victory. Mastery of opposing forces by decision and strength of will.

Description

A royal male figure driving a chariot. In most decks he is crowned, and usually wearing full armor. The chariot has a canopy so constructed that this figure is also between two pillars.

The chariot is pulled by two beasts, which may be either real or mystical—horses, sphinxes, sometimes unicorns or winged horse-like creatures. In some decks, the two draft animals are opposite colors (as white and black). In most, if not all, decks they appear to be moving in opposite directions (one to the right, one to the left), yet both pulling the same chariot. This symbolizes aspects of your own nature which may work in opposition to each other, but are driving toward the same goal, as in your spiritual and physical natures. They also represent the opposing forces that you reconciled and mastered in the last stage of your progress (Arcanum Six), now being used to pull you forward to victory.

The meaning of this card is stronger than that of The Lovers. Where Arcanum Six depicts a union of apparent opposites, The Chariot pictures mastery of real opposites, control over and use of those things which are by their nature in conflict.

Meaning

Having reconciled the opposites within yourself to the point where you are able to draw on them at need, you are now in a position to overcome your real enemies.

Just as a chariot in battle runs down enemy forces, The Chariot in the Tarot symbolizes victory over all who oppose you. These are not elements (as in Arcanum Six) that can be made to reconcile and work together. They are forces which are by their nature enemies: good and evil, positive and negative, right and wrong. In some cases, they may still be factors within yourself which you must force to work in tandem, if not in agreement. Just as often, these opposing forces represent people or events in your life which are working to prevent you from reaching your goals.

Because you have drawn strength from the opposites within yourself by making them work together, you can now recognize your true enemies and use their own weaknesses—and your strength—against them. This is the victory The Chariot pictures. All your enemies have been confounded; all your aims have been fulfilled; nothing can stand in the way of your success.

The level of The Chariot is another point where it is very tempting for the seeker to stop. After all, you have not only made peace with yourself, but you have overcome everything in your way to reach and master a major goal. In fact, what you have achieved is important enough that it may seem to be the goal you were seeking, or even the only goal worth seeking. It can be very difficult to convince yourself that there is even more you can accomplish, if you will only continue your search.

In the Reading

Upright (or Positive): Conquest. Triumph over enemies or obstacles. May sometimes mean revenge. Victory over great odds; also, mastery of opposing forces. Can also mean that you will receive help or advice in a moment of great need (like the cavalry coming over the hill).

Reversed (or Negative): Conflict, war, trouble. Defeat or disharmony. Quarrels, disputes. Being overpowered by enemies or obstacles.

The Chariot offers you the means to take what you've learned so far and use it to overcome anyone or anything trying to prevent you from reaching your goals. If this card represents the querent, then whether or not you are aware of it, you are now in a position to defeat your enemies and force them to accept your terms. Look within yourself. The strength is there.

This is divine justice as opposed to human justice: absolutely impartial and strictly fair.

JUSTICE

La Justice (Justice). Corresponding to the number Eight, also to the Hebrew letter Cheth.

[Note: Waite and Grey show this card as number eleven, and Strength as number eight. In most decks, however, this card is shown as number eight.]

Represents

Impartial and unbiased justice. Strict fairness.

Description

A female figure, either standing or seated. In most decks, she is also shown between two pillars. She is crowned, and in some decks wearing armor, in others wearing robes. In one hand she holds a sword upright; in the other, she holds scales in perfect balance.

The important imagery in this card is that Justice in the Tarot, unlike the Lady Justice in modern imagery, is *not* blindfolded. Her eyes are large and open, and she looks straight out at the viewer. Divine Justice is not blinded by human limitations.

Meaning

This is divine justice as opposed to human justice—absolutely impartial and strictly fair. She stands in direct contradiction to human justice which is influenced by factors that make it imperfect. True justice, divine justice, cannot be swayed by either influence or personal preferences, or by the simple limitations of human ability to judge between right and wrong. That which should be, will be, and no one can change it.

Her scales are absolutely in balance, and she sees clearly what must be done. The sword in one hand and the scales in the other symbolize the dual nature of Justice: accuracy and severity.

In this stage of your spiritual development, this is the type of vision that is required of you to learn as an initiate. To pass through these portals you must learn to look outward at the world and inward at yourself without bias, with your eyes open, seeing only and precisely what is there, rather than what you want to see, or hope to see, and judging it only and exactly for what it truly is.

In the Reading

Upright (or Positive): Equity. Victory of the right in general; also, triumph for the deserving side in legal matters. Ability to judge without being swayed by personal considerations or bias. Fairness, reasonableness, proper balance. Impartiality. This card also indicates (and sometimes influences) lawsuits and legal matters.

Reversed (or Negative): Bigotry, inequality, bias. Abuse of justice, complications in legal affairs. Unfair punishment; excessive severity.

This is Justice as an ideal—to do what is right despite opposition, or personal inclination, or the vagaries of human law. If this card represents a situation, you will get what you deserve; the outcome will be what is strictly fair and absolutely right under the circumstances. If this card represents the querent, then your perception of the situation in which you find yourself, or of the people you're dealing with, is absolutely accurate. You have made, or are capable of making, the correct decision here. Don't let anyone convince you otherwise.

The imagery here is of a search, done alone, and requiring light (the lantern representing understanding or knowledge) to discover its goal.

THE HERMIT

L'Ermite (The Hermit). Corresponding to the number Nine, also to the Hebrew letter Teth.

Represents

Self-examination. A vision quest.

Description

An old man, usually bearded, dressed in robes. The robes here, however, are very plain and unadorned, though they may also hint at the deck's religious affiliation: Egyptian or Old Testament garments, medieval monk's robes in some decks, in others the kind worn in Wiccan Circle. The robe is often hooded and may be bound at the waist by a knotted cord.

The Hermit is always standing; in most decks, he is also walking. Any background shows desert or other open spaces, though there may be mountains in the far distance. He carries a lantern in one hand, held out before him to light the way; in some decks, he may also be leaning on a staff.

The imagery here is of a search, done alone, and requiring light (the lantern representing understanding or knowledge) to discover its goal. The Hermit takes nothing with him but what he has; he requires no trappings of royalty or position (the plain robe). He has only the need to complete his search—and the means within himself to accomplish that goal.

Meaning

Almost all religions have their own legends of a vision quest, or of a great teacher or prophet who searches the world seeking truth—or God.

The Hermit teaches that there comes a point in your spiritual self-development when you must withdraw from the temptations and demands of civilization and go out into the desert to search your soul for the meaning of your own existence—and to find your God. The Deity cannot speak clearly to you when you're distracted by the demands of day-to-day existence. The search for truth must be pursued alone.

This is as much a search for Self as for God, but the imagery suggests that you will receive divine inspiration in your search, if it is an honest one. The lantern represents your own knowledge and understanding, which you must use to light your way in your search. The staff may be understood to represent God, a strength you can lean on to keep you steady throughout your search, and protection against enemies you may meet on the way. Leaving behind the trappings of civilization and seeking only for the truth, The Hermit allegorizes the experience of self-initiation.

In the Reading

Upright (or Positive): Self-examination, moderation, wisdom, silence. Hidden truth. Prudence, withdrawal, circumspection, caution, solitude. Learning through experience; a seeker. May also foretell an upcoming journey.

Reversed (or Negative): Deception, lies, misinformation. Corruption, concealment. Misguided ideals. Disguise or even fraud.

As Arcanum Eight depicts Justice in its pure form, Arcanum Nine is a search for truth in its pure form, uncorrupted by ideologies, preferences, or needs. If this card represents the querent, then you are going through, or are about to undergo, a period of self-examination. This will be a time when you re-evaluate your life, your associations, and your goals. The possible changes that this will create in your life (and/or possible conclusions you may arrive at) will be suggested by the other cards in the reading.

MEDICINE WHEEL

The Wheel of Fortune teaches you that there are things in life that just happen, and over which not you, and not even Blind Fate herself, have any real control.

WHEEL of FORTUNE.

XI WHEEL OF FORTUNE

THE WHEEL OF FORTUNE

La Roue de Fortune (The Wheel of Fortune). Corresponding to the number Ten, also to the Hebrew letter Yod.

Represents

Chance. Blind fate. A situation over which you have no control.

Description

Most decks show a wheel whose axle is supported by two uprights; in some decks, the wheel is at the edge of a cliff. There are generally three figures on the wheel or bound to it; one at the top, one ascending the wheel, one descending. In some decks, the descending figure is falling off the wheel, usually over the cliff. The figures on the wheel may be either human or animal; if animal, they have some kind of symbolic form, such as a sphinx, or clothed, monkey-like beings. The figure at the top of the wheel is depicted as significant in some way— crowned, or bearing a sword, or evidently celebrating.

In some decks the wheel stands alone, though it is obviously turning. In others, a blindfolded young woman is turning the wheel. Note that none of the figures on the wheel are aware of her, even the one who is falling. In fact, no one, including the blindfolded woman, is watching or really consciously controlling the results of the wheel's turns. In a few decks, the wheel is simply a disc suspended in the sky, with letters or symbols written around it. In these decks, in addition to the three figures bound to the wheel, there are also four symbolic figures in each of the corners of the card: at the top a human and a bird or griffin, at the bottom a lion and a bull. All four figures are winged.

Meaning

We are all bound to the Wheel of Fortune. Some of us are fighting our way upward; some of us fall by the wayside. Some sit on top of the heap, apparently unaffected by the vagaries of fortune. But the wheel is turning for everyone, whether or not we are aware of it. What results for everyone is pure chance, and has nothing to do with individual worth, or lack of it. The message here is in direct contrast to Justice (Arcanum Eight). In both cards, each individual is treated with strict impartiality. In Justice, however, the result is fair: you get what you deserve. In Fortune, you get whatever happens to come, no matter what you deserve. What's worse, the forces controlling your life don't consider you, or anyone else, at all; they don't even see you. In effect, you become like the objects on The Juggler's table, tossed about at random. In fact, you are even less than that, for at least The Juggler watches what he's working with, even if he doesn't care about anyone except himself.

Arcanum Ten teaches you that there are things in life that just happen, and over which not you, and not even Blind Fate herself, have any real control. You must be aware that the Wheel is constantly turning, and that your life is being affected by it. If you want success, you have to fight to take control of the uncontrollable; to force Fate to give you what you choose, whether or not you deserve it.

The secret of good fortune is to learn to use your psychic, or inner, powers to control your fate, rather than allowing yourself to be shifted around by any wind that blows. Blind Fortune has no interest in who wins or loses; she simply turns the Wheel at random. If you want to come out on top, you have to learn to care enough about what happens to you to take control of the Wheel of Fortune.

In the Reading

Upright (or Positive): Good luck. Destiny; fortune. Success. An unexpected turn of events. Promotion or elevation. Victory; obstacles overcome by good fortune.

Reversed (or Negative): Surplus of acquisitions, dragging at your coat tails. Failure. Bad luck, problems, unexpected harm.

Your future is being decided NOW. Take control of your life, or wind up wherever blind fortune chooses to send you. If this card represents the querent, then what is happening to you—good or bad—has nothing whatsoever to do with what you deserve. It's just happening. If you like it, let it proceed. If you don't, then fight it, but you are not being either punished or rewarded in this situation. In fact, you are not being considered at all.

STRENGTH

The Strength card symbolizes the inner strength required to overcome obstacles placed in your path.

VIII

STRENGTH.

VIII STRENGTH

Trumps Eleven

STRENGTH

La Force (Strength; or, Fortitude). Corresponding to the number Eleven, also to the Hebrew letter Kaph.

(Note: Waite and Gray show this card as number Eight, and Justice as Number Eleven. Most decks number the Major Arcana as shown here.)

Represents

Overcoming obstacles. Spiritual strength and force of will. Victory over overwhelming odds.

Description

Many decks show a young woman wrestling with a lion; she is fighting bare-handed and winning. In some decks it appears that she is closing the lion's mouth; in others, she is pulling its jaws apart.

Either way, she is forcing the lion to act according to her wishes rather than its own. In these decks, the infinity symbol (∞) is shown above the woman's head; sometimes it appears in the shape of her headpiece or hat.

A few decks show a strong young man wrestling bare-handed with a lion; he may represent a figure such as Heracles or Samson. In this case, the man's club is lying on the ground at his feet; either dropped or thrown down so that he can wrestle bare-handed. He may or may not be handling the lion's mouth in some way.

Where the card shows a male wrestling with the lion, there is definitely a battle in progress whose end is victory or death. Where the card shows a woman, it often appears that she is not so much wrestling with the lion as taming it, by the sheer force of her will.

In either case, the imagery is of a single individual winning over a much more powerful opponent with no weapon except his or her own fortitude and determination on which to rely.

Meaning

This card symbolizes the inner strength required to overcome obstacles placed in your path. Brute force is not conquered by brute force; rather, it is spiritual strength that overcomes physical strength. In almost all the legends of humans overcoming some powerful beast, be it a lion or a dragon, or anything else, victory is won by right, not by might—by the individual's inner fortitude and trust in God.

The beast in this case may represent external obstacles to your spiritual progress. It also represents the beast within, however, your own fears and passions, and other qualities within yourself which may seem to be stronger than you are, but which can be changed and tamed if you persist in the belief that it is you who are the stronger. The lion symbolizes any apparently unbeatable opponent which can be conquered if you have faith in yourself and the will to succeed. (Just as an example: anyone who has ever given up smoking, or stayed with a strict diet, has conquered this kind of beast.)

The allegory here is also, as mentioned above, of a battle between the physical and the spiritual. You are on the road to spiritual enlightenment. To achieve your ends, you must overcome or tame your base passions and force them to surrender to your higher self.

In the Reading

Upright (or Positive): Force of will, moral strength. Personal vitality. Courage, triumph. Fortitude, determination, energy, defiance. Ability to endure hardship. Success.

Reversed (or Negative): Abuse of power, despotism. Failure, disgrace. Weakness (either physical or spiritual), discord, lack of harmony.

You are facing a test of your endurance. If your will is stronger than whatever opponent you battle, you will survive and succeed. If not, your dreams end here. Fortitude is your key to victory; do not despair. If this card represents the querent, then you are facing a test of your own determination and will. The battle will not be an easy one, but you can win if you make up your mind to see this through. You will lose only if you choose to surrender.

THE HANGED MAN

*The Hanged Man
tells you that personal
sacrifice is required in
order to attain
your goal.*

THE HANGED MAN.

12 THE HANGED MAN

CASTLE PERILOUS

Trumps Twelve

∽∿∿

THE HANGED MAN

Le Pendu (The Hanged Man). Corresponding to the number Twelve, also to the Hebrew letter Lamed.

Represents

Self-sacrifice, with the object of attaining wisdom, special insights, or personal growth.

Description

A male figure hanging upside down from a kind of gallows. Sometimes two uprights are shown on either side of the figure, supporting the beam from which he hangs, a repetition of the theme of the two pillars, or doorway. Just as often, only the horizontal beam itself is shown. Note that if two uprights are shown, they are trimmed trees with roots in the living earth; if only the horizontal is shown, it has leaves at various points along its length. So in either case, the "gallows" from which he is suspended is living wood.

The Hanged Man is suspended by a leather or ribbon tie around one foot or ankle. His other foot dangles free and is bent behind the leg by which he is suspended. In most decks, his hands are either bound or clasped behind his back.

The point to note here is that this figure does not appear to be in any pain or distress. Some cards show a peaceful expression on his face, others contemplative, or even exalted, but it is evident that this particular ordeal is his own choice, and that he is getting from it whatever goal he is suffering it for.

Meaning

As with the Hermit (Arcanum Nine), many religions and myths describe a divine or semi-divine figure who chose to endure some form of personal sacrifice in order to attain divine wisdom or even godhood. In Norse myth, for example, Odin, ruler of the gods, hung for nine days and nights from the sacred tree, Yggdrasil, to attain the wisdom of the runes. In the case of the Hermit, seeking in solitude is the means to understanding your goal; in The Hanged Man, the message is that personal sacrifice is required of you in order to attain it.

The Hanged Man is not being sacrificed by or for others. The choice is his, and so are the rewards; that is the message here. There are goals for which you must perform some kind of personal sacrifice, that is, for which you must endure an uncomfortable or unpleasant experience. If you do, the benefits to you personally are well worth the price. (If others happen to benefit too, as in the case of Odin's runes, that's just icing on the cake—but it's not the reason for the sacrifice.)

The point is that the choice must be yours, and the sacrifice must be a willing one, because the goal is worth it to you. Both sacrifice and goal may be on any level; physical, intellectual, or spiritual. But whatever your goal, there is the need to sacrifice your childish or selfish illusions to achieve your adult dreams. Just as God created humans in the divine image, you must re-create your Self in the image of the man or woman you choose to be.

There is also another message in this card. The only person you are entitled to sacrifice to attain your goals is yourself.

In the Reading

Upright (or Positive): Self-sacrifice, growth of wisdom, intuition. Devotion, surrender, renunciation. Giving something up for the sake of something better. Prophecy.

Reversed (or Negative): Selfishness, self-interest. Political machinations. Petty sacrifices, lack of ties. May mean a loss of something you want or need.

The Hanged Man requires that you be willing to suffer some loss or surrender some pleasure in order to attain your goal. The greater the goal, the greater the sacrifice required to win it. If this card represents the querent, you are going to have to pay—and pay dearly—for whatever it is that you want. If you're willing to pay the price, you can attain your goal. Just remind yourself throughout this difficult time that the choice is yours: pay the price, or sacrifice the goal.

DEATH

❧

Death symbolizes a complete severence with the past; the ending of your life as it was.

❧

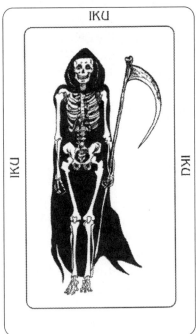

IKU

13 DEATH

GWYN AB NUDD
& THE WILD HUNT

Trumps Thirteen

DEATH

La Mort (Death). Corresponding to the number Thirteen, also to the Hebrew letter Mem.

Represents

Abrupt change; an end to things as they are or were. Death.

Description

In many decks, Death is pictured traditionally as a skeleton with a scythe. In some decks, Death may be depicted as a skeleton in black armor, riding a horse. The figure is sometimes grinning, sometimes appearing angry or vengeful.

Background also varies. Sometimes the ground is sparse and bare, as though the earth itself is dead. Other decks show parts of bodies: heads, hands, feet, and bones. Some decks show different degrees of people (a king, a maiden, a child, a priest), either already dead or facing death. The imagery here is that no one is spared, from the highest to the lowest.

Meaning

Death symbolizes a complete severance with the past, the ending of your life as it was. It can be interpreted as giving up old ideas, and old ways of acting. It can also be interpreted as a complete change in your life or lifestyle, a crossing over from one mode of existence to another. It also represents the end of close associations, either because you move on or others do.

Death's sickle symbolizes reaping; you have sown your seed, it has grown to this point, and now it is time for the harvest. You take what you have learned and move on to the next (and, if you've learned what you should, higher) stage of existence.

In any case, there is an actual death here, but with it the beginning of a new life. The Death card allegorizes the end of the person you were, but this is not something to fear. It's something you've earned; in fact, it is something you've worked for. The end of who and what you were comes because of the sacrifices you've made (Arcanaum Twelve) and all you've learned until now. From here you go on to a life completely different from anything you've known before, or can even imagine.

Though I haven't included numerological interpretations so far, it's important to at least touch on it in this case. The number thirteen is neither lucky nor unlucky in itself. It represents transformations—on the material plane, usually a change for the better—and rebirth: a boundary between what was and what will be.

In the Reading

Upright (or Positive): Sudden change; an end to things as they were. Mortality; inevitability. A situation or event that cannot be avoided. May mean actual death, your own or that of someone close to you, or sudden collapse of your plans. Failure.

Reversed (or Negative): Destruction, loss, failure of plans. Apathy, loss of hope or faith. Changes for the worse (though not necessarily fatal).

A major change is about to happen in your life. Whatever it is, good or bad, it cannot be avoided. Note that while this card represents a positive transformation in the stages of spiritual enlightenment, in a reading, it is a very unfavorable card.

If this card represents the querent, you are facing a complete break with your old life, and there is little or nothing you can do to stop it. Be sure to interpret the other cards in your reading carefully to determine exactly what that change is. It can mean anything from material change, such as divorce or loss of a job, to actual death. If the change is in your material status or relationships, being prepared may help you salvage something, or at least go on from there. If this card predicts your own death, or that of someone close to you, the other cards will tell you how and why it will come. There may be something you can do to prevent it (as in avoiding a deadly situation, or anticipating a potential suicide). Or it may simply mean that you can only accept and prepare for the inevitable.

EL ANGEL CUSTODIO

THE GUARDIAN ANGEL

O ANJO CUSTÓDIO

The lesson Temperance teaches is among the most important—and probably the most difficult—of lessons you need to learn: patience.

14 TEMPERANCE

THE CAULDRON OF ANNWN

XIV

TEMPERANCE.

TEMPERANCE

Temperance. Corresponding to the number Fourteen, also to the Hebrew letter Nun.

Represents

Patience, self-control, willingness to learn understanding.

Description

A winged angel stands by a stream. In some decks, the figure has one foot in the stream and one on the shore. The angel may be either male or female; it's not always possible to tell, nor does it matter. Some decks show the angel with a halo and/or a crown, or some form of symbolic disc worn on the forehead.

The angel holds two cups or pitchers, one in each hand, and is pouring liquid, probably water, from one to the other. The background shows countryside and mountains in the distance; in some decks, the stream (at the angel's feet) flows down from the mountains. Some decks also show a barely visible crown over the mountains.

The use of an angel as the primary figure in this card symbolizes the idea that we have the ability to raise ourselves to the angelic level, if we can learn the lesson Temperance teaches.

Meaning

The lesson this card teaches is among the most important—and probably the most difficult—of lessons you need to learn: patience. There are times in your life when it seems like nothing is happening, nothing is moving; you've come to a standstill, and there's nothing you can do about it.

This is not a matter of someone or something deliberately holding you up. It is a necessary waiting period, and though it may seem like a delay, things are happening. To use a very mundane example: Once you've made your batter, poured it in the pan and put it in the oven, you have to wait until it's baked. It does no good to pace up and down and frustrate yourself. There is a certain amount of time you MUST wait for your cake to bake properly. The fact remains that while you're waiting, the cake is baking. Efforts you have made, projects you have put into motion, are coming to fruition. You just have to be patient.

Temperance also teaches that you can make constructive use of those times when all you can do is wait. You use them to consider what you've done and what you will do, to explore your own needs and motives, to let learning become understanding.

Most important, however, you use them to force yourself to learn patience. We are so accustomed in this life to doing something. It is important to learn that there are times when there is simply nothing—or at least nothing more—you can or need to do.

In the Reading

Upright (or Positive): Patience, accommodation, moderation, frugality, temperance, reflection. Diplomacy; impartiality. Good management; economy. Ability to coordinate.

Reversed (or Negative): Disunion, lack of harmony. Competing interests; unfortunate combinations or alliances (such as socially unacceptable marriages or partnerships). Frustration, impatience.

Even though it seems you are stalled, things are proceeding toward their proper ends and will arrive in their proper time. Don't push it. There's nothing you can do right now. If this card represents the querent and you are impatient for results, the message is the same. If you are sitting back and waiting for results, then you're doing exactly the right thing. In fact, you're doing the only thing possible in this situation.

15

THE DEVIL

The allegory here is not independent will, but of an intelligence that works to destroy for the sake of upsetting the divine balance.

XV

THE DEVIL .

EL DIABLO

THE DEVIL

O DIABO

Trumps Fifteen

THE DEVIL

Le Diable (The Devil). Corresponding to the number Fifteen, also to the Hebrew letter Samekh.

Represents

The struggle between the supreme good and the supreme evil; a choice or conflict between order and chaos.

Description

Some decks show a traditional devil, complete with horns, hooves, tail and pitchfork. In these, he is shown exalting over a single weeping figure; his stance, with one arm raised like a puppet master, parodies the standing figure of the High Priest.

Most decks show a larger devil with two smaller figures, male and female, standing at the foot of his throne. The small figures may be demons, humans, or horned humans; in all such decks they are chained or tied to the foot of the Devil's throne. Note that the position of these three figures is an echo—or a mockery—of the illustration shown in Arcanum Five (The High Priest).

The central Devil figure in these decks may take a variety of forms, from the Horned Goat to a more human shape; he may be either an attractive figure or really frightening. Whatever his shape, in most cases he is also winged and horned; he sometimes wears the inverted pentagram on his brow or as a crown.

In almost all decks, The Devil has one hand upraised and/or extended over the two souls chained to his throne. The main figure is usually seated, but may be standing; his expression ranges from tempting smile to angry frown. His attitude directly affects the other two figures in the illustration. If The Devil is smiling, so are his two acolytes; if he is frowning, then his two slaves are either sorrowing or afraid.

Again, the imagery of this powerful figure whose gesture affects or controls those who come within its influence can be read as either a reverse or a sarcasm of the benediction given by the Hierophant in Arcanum Five. It can sometimes be difficult to tell whether the two smaller figures are his prisoners, his servants, or his pets; in any case, they are unquestionably bound to his will.

Note that by standing on either side of the main figure, and despite the fact that they are on a lower level and much smaller than the Devil, the two smaller figures not only echo the smaller priests of Arcanum Five, but are also in the position and thus echo the two pillars shown in other cards of this Arcana.

Meaning

The Devil represents the antithesis of good, the forces that strive to upset the harmonious order of existence. It is not simply being an individualist, or wanting his own way, that makes this being evil. The Magician (Arcanum One) also tries to impose his own will on the universe, and, in fact, one of the results of completing the Path of the Tarot is to enable you to truly control your own destiny.

The allegory here is not independent will, but of an intelligence that works to destroy for the sake of upsetting the divine balance. His purpose is to defeat Divine Law and return the world to a state of chaos.

The ancients taught that there is an order to the universe, within which all living beings could find their own best destiny. Divine Law seeks to establish and maintain that order; The Devil works to upset and undermine it. He may operate as a tempter, or he may command by fear, but either way his purpose is to offer irresistible inducements to stray from the true path.

The True Path, as taught by the Tarot, is to become as close to the divine as possible. At this stage in your spiritual development you have become adept enough to be a valuable servant for the forces of evil. This is the point at which you can chose either to continue toward your ultimate goal, or take the left-hand path, which ends here. The inducements are especially tempting to the seeker at this time. You've just been forced to wait for fulfillment of your purpose(s) (Temperance). The Devil seems to offer a way to achieve those purposes without any more waiting, or any further work.

The power offered is tremendous, but the price demanded is even greater. Never forget that you can achieve your goals without The Devil's help. In fact, the only reason he's interested in you is because your potential exceeds anything he can hope to achieve—unless he can stop you.

You are not being offered an easier way. The significance of the chained figures teaches that what you must surrender to take the power The Devil offers is your own free will.

In the Reading

Upright (or Positive): Hatred, violence, destruction. Turmoil, fatality, bad luck. Willing bondage. Your own authority and will removed and given to another. Also, that which is predestined and therefore unescapable, but not for that reason necessarily evil.

Reversed (or Negative): Pettiness, weakness. Blindness, jealousy, illness. Evil fate. Wrong choices. Disaster for you which benefits others.

You're being offered a quick fix for your problems. If you are impatient enough to take it, you may see the destruction of all your dreams and plans. You can succeed on your own. Don't be tempted by shortcuts, however attractive; or dismayed by the hard work involved if you continue alone.

If this card represents the querent, beware. The power you are exercising over your subordinates is heady, and you may find it satisfying to manipulate, control, and even destroy their lives. But even the real Devil has no place to go but down.

THE TOWER.

This card represents destruction resulting directly from your own lack of understanding and good judgement, and/or from the misuse of your free will.

16 THE TOWER

VORTIGERN'S FORTRESS

XVI THE TOWER

Trumps Sixteen

THE FALLING TOWER

La Maison de Dieu (The House of God; also the Falling Tower, or the Tower of Destruction). Corresponding to the number Sixteen, also to the Hebrew letter Ayin.

Represents

A setback; the ruin of all your plans; disaster resulting from your own misuse of power or divine gifts.

Description

A stone fortress or tower; the top of it is sometimes shown as a crown. The tower is being struck by lightning from the heavens, which represents divine wrath. The top of the tower is sheared off, and the tower itself is falling to pieces. Debris and sparks are falling from the tower. The illustration also shows two human figures, usually both male, falling to their deaths from the top of the tower.

The allegory here is of a construction representing human power and vanity being destroyed by divine wrath.

Meaning

The most familiar story corresponding to the symbolism in this card is that of the Tower of Babel. The people of Babel came very close to accomplishing what could be humanity's greatest goal: a complete unity of purpose. They all spoke one language; they all worked together to accomplish one end. The result of their cooperation was that their work was destroyed, their language was confused, and they were scattered to the four corners of the earth.

It's important to understand that it was not the actual building of the tower that was wrong; and certainly not the fact that they cooperated in building it. Where they erred was in the reason the tower was built. Rather than using their united strength to reach toward the divine in themselves, they used it to challenge God and to attempt to rule the earth in God's stead.

This card follows from Arcanum Fifteen (The Devil). The purpose of your path toward spiritual self-enlightenment is to become like God. But, says the Tarot, you don't become like God simply by having power over the material plane. If you are tempted by the possibilities in controlling this world instead of striving for wisdom and spiritual growth, you will lose all you gained. The reason for the disaster is not because you developed great powers, but because you misused them. It is destruction resulting directly from your own lack of understanding and good judgement, and/or from the misuse of your free will.

The Falling Tower can represent actual material loss, as in finances, relationships, prestige or personal influence. It can also be understood as a warning that your powers are not as great, or your understanding of them as complete, as you believe. In this sense, it illustrates the disaster which can and does happen to those who use magick without understanding its true purposes, the destruction of the person who plays with powers beyond their control or understanding.

In the spiritual sense, The Falling Tower symbolizes the result for the seeker if you take the path The Devil offered—even though, in this case, you strike out on your own to do it.

Although it has been hinted at along the way, this is the first direct statement in the Tarot of how you must view your ultimate goal. It is not this world you are trying to conquer.

At this point in your search, it is still tempting to evaluate success according to the terms of this world, to impress others, to rule this plane, or in some other way to attain mundane status. What makes it even more tempting is that you now have attained the power to twist the world to your will—at least for a time. But your goal is greater than that. You must learn to see beyond the obvious to a higher level of attainment. If you surrender your spiritual progress for material power, you will lose everything you've gained.

In the Reading

Upright (or Positive): Disruption, adversity, calamity, misery, deception. Unforeseen ruin, termination. Disgrace, misery. A financial or personal loss, such as the destruction of your home or business, the breakup of a marriage or relationship, any disastrous change in your personal or financial affairs; in particular, an unforeseen catastrophe.

Reversed (or Negative): Still foretells calamities and losses, but of a lesser importance in your life; they will disrupt your life while they're going on, but they don't mean the end of everything you've built. A sudden, unexpected change. Oppression, adversity, deception, tyranny.

That which you have built is ending in disaster. In most cases, these disasters could have been prevented had you acted wisely to begin with. If you act wisely now, you may be able to alleviate at least some of the problems about to occur.

If this card represents the querent, you've overstepped yourself and are about to pay the price. But even in this case, it is not a punishment for hubris. It is disaster resulting from the fact that you believed you had powers or authority that in fact you don't, or because you used your powers or authority unwisely or for the wrong reasons. In simple terms: you blew it, and your resulting downfall is your own fault.

THE STAR

The allegory of the Star card is not of simple patience, but of putting back something of yourself.

THE STAR.

XVII THE STARS

Trumps Seventeen

THE STAR

L'Etoile (The Star). Corresponding to the number Seventeen, also to the Hebrew letter Pe.

Represents

Wisdom, immortality, accomplishment of your goals, generosity and understanding.

Description

A female figure kneels on one knee at the edge of a stream. In most decks, her knee is on the land and her other foot is in the stream. She is holding two pitchers, one in each hand, from which she is emptying the water. In all decks, she is pouring water from at least one of those pitchers back into the stream; in many decks, the water from the second pitcher is being poured onto the ground beside the stream, and only some of it returns to the stream. Note the corresponding imagery to Arcanum Fourteen (Temperance). But the allegory here is not of simple patience (ie: occupying yourself while waiting for a goal to come to fruition), but of putting back something of yourself.

Above her head there are stars, though their number and arrangement varies from deck to deck. Some decks show seven stars, arranged in a circle over her head, in a halo-like effect. Other decks show seven smaller stars in various configurations, and one much larger star which is always directly over the figure's head. Often the decks which show this second symbolism configure the smaller stars in two columns on either side of the larger star, echoing the portal theme. There are also decks which show only the larger star, again, directly over the woman's head.

The background shows an open, country-like setting. Many decks show one or two trees in the distance, with a bird alighting on the topmost branches of one tree. If there are two trees shown, they are on either side of the figure, just as the columns in other cards of this Arcana.

The significant symbolism is that the woman is pouring water back into the stream. She is returning to its source a portion of what she has or was given.

Meaning

Consider the imagery of the stars. From earliest times, people have been fascinated and guided by these signs in the heavens. Astrology teaches that the positions of the stars influences our lives, but even those with no knowledge of Astrology pay heed to these distant beacons. Travelers use the North Star (or, below the equator, the Southern Cross) to find their way. People have always seen pictures in the arrangement of the stars and created legends about them. Now, in our own time, the stars take on yet another important meaning as slowly but surely we make our way toward them.

The stars represent the universe in all its mystery and potential for growth, learning, and power. They symbolize what is out there, still on the material plane, but yet beyond the confines of this world. In many ways, not just in Astrology, the stars direct our lives. In this Arcanum, the seeker is given the opportunity to assume control of that direction.

Just as The Tower (Arcanum Sixteen) showed the disastrous results of power used unwisely, The Stars shows the potential of that wisdom and understanding which is true power. Greek myth relates that the Olympian deities set humans among the stars to immortalize them. Arcanum Seventeen shows the beginning of your own immortality.

At this point in your quest, you become a teacher as well as a seeker. The stars arrange themselves at your direction, giving you the power that The Magician only attempts to employ: to be at the center of the universe, to change the heavens at your will.

But to gain and keep this power, you must put something back. The young woman in this picture is pouring the life force, symbolized by the water, back into the earth plane, even as the stars above her head arrange themselves to pour their power into her. It is the beginning of a transformation: the stars above her do what she does, because she is beginning to become what they are. It is a prime example, if a different definition than The Magician's, of "as above, so below."

The young woman represents eternal youth and true beauty. The stars above her symbolize the potential to achieve your goals—and, more importantly, true understanding of what those goals should be. The water in the stream symbolizes serenity (greater than patience); born of the knowledge that you will overcome all obstacles. It is a generous portion of both her knowledge and her power that she returns to the earth to revitalize that from which she sprang. The stars teach that even as you prepare to go on to a higher plane of knowledge and achievement, it is important to remember that your roots—and therefore the basis of your strength—are in this plane. You must consider not only where you are going, but those who will come after you.

In the Reading

Upright (or Positive): Wisdom, immortality, spiritual enlightenment. Hope, happiness, intellectual fulfillment. Satisfaction, hope, bright prospects, destiny, insight. Progress toward your goals; understanding of what those goals should be.

Reversed (or Negative): Frustration, impotence, theft. Unfulfilled expectations, disappointments, abandonment. Arrogance leading to losses instead of gains.

You have found the path which will enable you to achieve your own form of immortality, however you may define it. Use your power wisely, serene in the knowledge that that which you seek is within your grasp. If this card represents the querent, what you have or are about to accomplish will enable you to make your mark on the world. You need no longer fear any rivals; no one has the ability or even potential to

take this success from you. If you are wise and generous, you will also realize that you can increase your
influence and the memory of your name by teaching at
least some of what you have learned to others.

The Moon tells you that you want to learn to shape events, not be shaped by them.

THE MOON

La Lune (The Moon). Corresponding to the number Eighteen, also to the Hebrew letter Tzaddik.

Represents

Mystery, intuition, psychic ability, deception and danger.

Description

This is usually a divided card. The upper half shows the moon at top center. It is within a full circle, but the moon is actually a crescent, increasing to what is called the "side of mercy" (to the right of the observer); in effect, the moon is shown in both its crescent and full form. There is a face in the moon, on the left side of the crescent, looking down at the scene below. In some decks, the full circle is rayed; where there are rays around the moon, there are usually also water-drop shapes falling from the moon onto the earth below, symbolizing the descent of spirit into matter.

[Note that the crescent and disc is a very ancient representation of the moon deity. Ancient steles (monuments bearing inscriptions) from the Mideast, inscribed in Aramaic and Phonecian, repeatedly show the symbol in this form (with the crescent inside the disc); in North Africa, specifically the area which was the center of Punic culture, the disc was shown inside (or suspended below) the crescent. In any case, it is direct archaeological evidence that at least some of the symbolism of the Major Arcana is much older than fourteenth or fifteenth century European culture.]

Also in the upper half of the picture, below the moon, there are two towers on either side of the picture (again, echoing the portal theme). Two animals, usually a dog and a wolf, are positioned between the towers, howling up at the moon. They represent our animal nature, both fascinated by and fearful of the effects of the moon, but ever affected by it rather than controlling it.

In the bottom half of the picture there is a pool or lake, from which is climbing a lobster, crab, or crayfish. (It is probably a crab, the sign of Cancer.) The symbolism here, as in the droplets descending from the moon, is of water, which is of course also affected by the cycles of the moon.

The illustration shows that while there is power to be derived from the moon, stronger than that is the pull of the moon, its control over the earth and our selves. Again, water is the life force, but in this case, what is emphasized is its fluidity: its ability to take on the shape of whatever container it is in.

This is the danger you must avoid: you want to learn to shape events, not be shaped by them.

Meaning

There is tremendous power to be gained here, but there is also a danger of which the seeker must always be aware. The Moon represents the lure of the unknown, hidden knowledge, truth obscured. A lack of complete information causes misunderstanding and conflicts, and makes it difficult if not impossible to arrive at correct conclusions. Be sure you understand exactly what you want and what you're doing before making your next move. Also be aware that the word "lunacy" comes from the word for moon, *luna*: there is the danger here of madness, desperation, even suicidal tendencies. All these things can interfere with your search for the hidden knowledge and power which is also contained in all aspects of The Moon.

The Moon has a magnetism which attracts and controls. It speaks to our animal nature, and draws on the subconscious, inducing volition without conscious thought. The only way to avoid its dangerous aspects is to deliberately assume conscious control: you must resist its pull and retain your own control. In short, to avoid the dangers in this card, you must learn to use your mind, your conscious intelligence, at all times. You may not surrender to your instincts; you dare not give in to your emotions. You are learning, in the paths of the Tarot, to draw on your subconscious and develop your psychic abilities. But this is the point at which you must put those abilities under conscious control. What differentiates people from animals (which are affected by the moon without knowing why) or from non-conscious elements (like the sea, which is affected by the moon without thinking at all) is our intelligence. Use your intelligence now, and from now on, or fail in your quest. You can no longer operate solely on your instincts.

In the Reading

Upright (or Positive): Caution, hidden danger, hidden enemies. Scandal, error, disillusionment, deception, strife. Also: intuition, latent psychic abilities possessed by the querent, occult forces in operation around you.

Reversed (or Negative): Deception and danger to a lesser degree of importance. Instability, unimportant errors, silence.

There are hidden forces of tremendous power operating around you. You may not be able to control them, but you can avoid being controlled by them. *Watch your step.*

If this card represents the querent, then you are being told that, whether or not you are aware of it, you possess tremendous psychic ability, most of it latent. Up until now, you have probably made little or no use of this ability. This is the best time for you to develop and learn to control it; you will need it in the times ahead. But act wisely. Either your misuse of this ability, or your refusal to use it at all, can lead you dangerously astray.

THE SUN

The Sun card symbolizes the transition between the visible light of this world, and the spiritual light of the world for which you are striving.

19 THE SUN

LLEU

XIX THE SUN

THE SUN

Le Soleil (The Sun). Corresponding to the number Nineteen; also to the Hebrew letter Quoph.

Represents

Happiness, contentment, success. Fulfillment. Gifts received.

Description

At the center top of the picture is a large sun, usually with a face looking out at the observer and always with beams radiating out from it. Some decks also show droplets raining down. Just as in The Moon card, this shows the descent of spirit into matter.

The scene below varies. Some decks show two young children, seated with their arms around each other, or a young male and female couple standing in a circle and holding hands. Other decks show two children standing together before a seawall—a Gemini-type representation. In still other decks, there is only one child, seated on a horse and obviously very happy. Again, there is a stone or brick wall behind him (her?); beyond the wall are large sunflowers.

However the figures are represented, the general feel of the illustration is of contentment, peace and safety, even joy. That it is children in these illustrations symbolizes a childlike (not childish!) happiness; the ability to simply enjoy life's gifts as they are given.

In The Moon card, you were warned to make full use of your adult intelligence and reasoning ability in order to survive. In this card, you can simply bask in the rays of a warm summer sun and enjoy the results of your accomplishments and what you are being freely given.

Meaning

The Moon shines with reflected light, and not enough light to illuminate hidden knowledge. But the Sun, however, is the source of light, bringing brightness and warmth, illuminating understanding, giving comprehension, clarity, and happiness.

Halfway between Heaven and Earth, The Sun serves as the mediator between God and humanity. It is at the same time the lowest aspect of the divine, and the highest aspect of the mundane. The Sun card symbolizes the transition between the visible light of this world and the spiritual light of the world for which you are striving. If you can approach the gifts it offers with the heart of a child—which has its own wisdom in innocence, simplicity and simple enjoyment of life—you take your next step toward the divine.

This is not an injunction to stop using your mind! Far from it. Children are constantly learning. What it is, is an injunction to follow the teachings of your heart as well. You are being given a great gift. What you have learned up until now allows you to simply enjoy it without the need to analyze it.

The lesson taught here is also one that may be as difficult to put into practice as that of Temperance (Arcanum Fourteen). Through all the stages of your search thus far, you have been under the necessity of striving and growing toward a very important goal. The Sun teaches that sometimes it's necessary to stop and smell the roses. You are permitted to enjoy what you've learned and what you are becoming!

As midpoint between the divine and material planes, The Sun allegorizes the seeker's identification with and appreciation of life in the here and now, as well as the hope and possibility of lives to come in a higher state of being.

In the Reading

Upright (or Positive): Triumph, success, happiness, accomplishment, contentment. Achievement; success and honors. A new beginning, a birth (as of a child, a project, an idea, a career). Material blessings, a joining (such as marriage) which will be happy.

Reversed (or Negative): All the same things, but to a lesser degree. This is never a negative card.

You can see your way clearly now. That which you have worked so hard for is about to come to fruition. You may even receive gifts which you haven't earned and perhaps didn't even expect.

Don't analyze them; don't question them; don't pick them into little pieces trying to figure out what they really mean. Just accept and enjoy them.

If this card represents the querent: You've worked very hard; you deserve to enjoy what you've earned, and what you've been given. Take the time now to at least sample the fruits of your labors. There's nothing wrong with taking pride in what you've accomplished—and getting some fun out of it as well. If you don't already know this basic truth, then now is the time you must make yourself learn it: You don't live to work. You work to live.

Savor your life. If you can't, there's no point in living it.

JUDGEMENT

Judgement symbolizes the end of your old life and the beginning of a new one, but in this case, whatever change is about to happen will be for the better.

EL KARMA

KARMA

O KARMA

XX JUDGMENT

Trumps Twenty

JUDGEMENT

Le Jugement (Judgement, or The Last Judgement). Corresponding to the number Twenty, also to the Hebrew letter Resh.

Represents

Final decisions made; a new life beginning; results, outcomes, conclusions. The end of your doubts; answers to your questions.

Description

At the top of the picture a divine figure, usually represented as a winged angel, leans down from a cloud, blowing on a trumpet. Below, nude human figures rise out of coffins or out of the earth itself, their faces expressing wonder and awe.

The number of human figures on the card may vary from three to six. They include both men and women and sometimes children as well. In some decks, the people stand in a circle with their hands clasped together; in others their arms are raised toward the angel, or there may be a combination of both attitudes. Other than those slight variations, most decks show a similar illustration.

The symbolism this card represents is that of the raising of the dead, the Last Judgement. This is the time when all souls will be called to account for their actions during their life's journeys, and when they will finally be told what they can expect as a result.

Note the use of the future tense here, however. They have not been told yet; they are simply receiving assurance that they will be told. The allegory is that of an awakening. And what they find upon waking is that the beliefs they held that brought them to this point were based on fact. There is indeed something beyond this life worth striving for.

Meaning

Like the Death card, Judgement symbolizes the end of your old life and the beginning of a new one. But in this case, whatever change is about to happen will be for the better. Your questions will be answered; your doubts resolved. You will know the truth at last.

These answers may happen on either the spiritual or the mundane plane of your life. On the mundane, for example, it may be that you can expect a new career, a new romance, a change for the better in your general lifestyle.

On the spiritual level, the answers are even more important. Up until now, you have been striving toward a goal sustained only by your faith that it must exist and that it's worth striving for.

Now you will be shown that it does in fact exist, and that nothing could be more worth striving for. Judgement promises the reward for your faith and your striving: proof that there is a reason and a purpose for both your existence and that of the universe from which you sprang, and through which you moved to reach this goal. From now on, you no longer have to believe. You know. Note that despite the type of illustration used here, this card does not actually refer to the Last Judgement in the sense of the end of the entire world. But it does mean the end of an old world for the seeker: and what is coming to an end is puzzlement, despair, and doubt. Judgement is a positive card, symbolizing regeneration, rebirth, understanding. Most importantly, you have a right to these rewards, because you earned them by your faith and your striving despite doubts. It is by our personal behavior and character that we are judged.

In the Reading

Upright (or Positive): Determination, decision, result, outcome. An introduction; a fresh start, a new beginning. Expect news, an important announcement, which will positively affect your progress. Problems resolved; questions answered. Change, rebirth, renewal: a radical but positive change in your life or circumstances.

Reversed (or Negative): Delay, deliberation, results postponed, weakness, cowardice. Also possibly punishment for any or all of these traits.

You've been stumbling blindly toward your goals; now is the time when your success and understanding is assured. Don't be afraid. Grasp this opportunity with both hands. If you delay, if you hesitate, the greatest opportunity of your life may slip through your fingers.

If this card represents the querent, be assured that you have been on the right track all along. No matter what doubts you may have had—or may still have— and no matter what negative feedback you may have received along the way, you did in fact make exactly the right choices for your own life and the lives of any others who were affected by those choices. Expect positive results very soon. Important questions will be answered, assurances received, doubts resolved. You will be rewarded for your efforts.

THE WORLD

The World symbolizes complete mastery and understanding of your own inner nature and of the forces surrounding you.

THE WORLD.

XXI UNIVERSE

Trumps Twenty-One

THE WORLD

Le Monde (The World). Corresponding to the number Twenty-One, also to the Hebrew letter Tav.

[Note: Waite's deck places The Fool here (though this card is still numbered Twenty-one, and The Fool is still numbered Zero). In terms of correspondence to the Hebrew alphabet, inserting The Fool here is correct; Tav is the last letter of the alphabet, and Shin (the letter corresponding to The Fool) second to the last. However, most decks do not interrupt the progress of the Arcana; they place The Fool at either the beginning or the end.]

Represents

Perfection, attainment. Your goals have been reached, your development or learning (in this area) is completed.

Description

In almost all decks, the central figure is a young nude woman, draped modestly with a long flowing scarf. She is surrounded by a wreath, made of either leaves, or leaves and flowers. In some decks, she is holding wands or staffs in both hands. The position of her hands varies; but a few decks show her gesturing in the same manner as The Magician: one hand upward, the other pointing down.

At the four corners of the card there are four different figures: upper left, a winged human or angel, upper right a hawk or eagle, lower left a bull, lower right a lion. Some decks show only the faces of these four figures; others show enough of the figures so that you can see that all four have wings. Note that the positioning of these four figures is similar to those sometimes found in Arcanum Ten (The Wheel of Fortune).

Meaning

This is the last numbered card of the Major Arcana. In this representation, you are the adept you have tried to become throughout your journey. Your transmutation (shown in the previous card, Judgement) is complete, and you have achieved the perfect synthesis of body (material), mind (intelligence), soul (self-awareness), and spirit (subconscious).

The World symbolizes complete mastery and understanding of your own inner nature and of the forces surrounding you. You know what is good and right in the universe and understand its intended order. And you can trust your judgement regarding what actions to take in the circumstances currently surrounding you. You have attained the status of a full adept.

This card is the reverse of the Falling Tower. In Arcanum Sixteen, destruction resulted from misuse of power; the failed adept assumed an authority which he or she did not in fact have, and reached for a goal to which he or she had no right.

But here, you attain an even greater goal than anything you could have wished for, or even imagined, at that earlier level.

There is no possibility of destruction, because it is no longer possible for you to make wrong choices. Everything you do is right. And you have a right to everything you have. You know who and what you are; you know why you are; and you know the reason for existence. And all of these answers serve to prove your own individual worth. This is the reward for your efforts.

In the Reading

Upright (or Positive): Completion, perfection, synthesis, ultimate change. Honesty and truth; assured success, harmony, attainment. Graduation; completion of a cycle. Recognition, reward, acclaim.

Reversed (or Negative): Negation, sacrifice of love or goals. Flight. Stagnation, inertia. Payback for evil deeds.

You have learned the lessons required for this incarnation (or situation, if the question involves mundane things). You are what you need to be; you know all you need to know; you have accomplished all you need to accomplish. You can now go on to other things, knowing that this task has been completed to perfection.

If this card represents the querent, you have achieved the ultimate success in your endeavor, and without any of the drawbacks that lesser successes so often bring. Everything you do, everything that happens, will only serve to prove your worth in this area.

But there is one caution. At this level of attainment, there is no place or need for further development in this area. But someone who has accomplished what you have accomplished cannot just sit back and do nothing with it. If you sit on your laurels, rather than finding another area to grow in, the result will be stagnation. As above, the job is done; it's time to move on.

THE FOOL.

The Fool represents someone walking blindly to his fate without heeding any warning signs along the way.

EL EXPULSADO

THE OUTCAST

O EXPULSO

0 THE FOOL

Trumps Zero

THE FOOL

Le Mat (The Fool). Corresponding to the number Zero, also to the Hebrew letter Shin.

[Note: Waite's deck places The Fool between Judgement (XX) and The World (XXI). Paul Case puts the Fool at the beginning of the Major Arcana, as do a number of others. MacGregor Mathers places it here, at the end, as do many others. This card, which may possibly be the most important in the Major Arcana, is definitely one for which you will have to make your own decision as to where it properly belongs. I've placed it at the end, because in order to make such a decision, you will also have to determine what you consider to be the correct interpretation of this card. And at this point, you know enough about the Tarot to do so.]

Represents

Unavoidable mistakes, due to your own (often deliberate) ignorance. Complete folly.

Description

A male figure stands at the edge of a cliff. He is walking toward the edge of the cliff, but not watching where he is going. He may be either looking back over his shoulder or staring up into the sky, but while his next step will take him over the edge of the cliff, he is totally unaware of his danger.

In some decks, The Fool is dressed in the parti-colored costume and cap and bells of a court jester; in others, he's wearing the plain and sometimes travel-worn costume of a wanderer. In most decks, The Fool carries a hobo's sack on a stick over one shoulder, and may or may not be leaning on a traveler's staff (like The Hermit, Arcanum Nine). Many decks also show a small dog in the picture, raised up on its hind legs and either barking at the figure, or actually grabbing at his clothes with its teeth to pull him back. Whatever the case, the dog is attempting to give The Fool warning of his danger. The Fool is so involved in his own thoughts, however, that he is paying no attention to the warning either.

It is important to note that it's not always clear, in this card, if the young man is actually a fool and about to take this dangerous step without knowing what he's doing, or if he is in fact aware of his danger and simply has no fear of it. In either case, the step he is about to take is a very drastic one.

The point to remember is that his folly is deliberate. Even starting the Path of the Tarot requires a blind leap of faith. There is no guide at all for what lies beyond it.

Meaning

Don't underestimate The Fool. He may appear to be a ridiculous figure. But you need to understand the lesson he teaches.

The overt symbolism in this card is of unmitigated folly. Like The Hermit (Arcanum Nine), The Fool is a traveler. But rather than using his own intelligence, or any other aid, to light his way, he is deliberately refusing to watch where he's going.

Note also the imagery relative to Arcanum Ten (The Wheel of Fortune). Like the figure falling off the Wheel, The Fool is headed over the edge of a cliff; but where in that case it is blind and uncaring Fate that causes that disaster, in this case, it is your own blind folly.

In mundane terms, The Fool describes the individual who is so determined to travel down a particular road no matter what that he is going out of his way to ignore all warning signs, or even watch his step. With that attitude, says Arcanum Zero, it is inevitable that you will walk blindly into making a really stupid mistake.

In terms of your personal development, The Fool tells you that you are missing the point—and in fact walking into very great danger because of it—simply because you refuse to see the truth which is right in front of you.

However, in terms of your progress through the Path of the Tarot, there are two possible interpretations for this card. If The Fool does in fact belong at the beginning of the Major Arcana, then the message is that you are a fool because you have not yet started your progress toward spiritual self-enlightenment. Without the understanding that such a study brings, you walk blindly through life, missing all the important signs and warnings, missing the point of life at all. Further, should you attempt to walk this road without watching where you're going (i.e.: to use the skills of an adept without understanding where they can lead you), you could be headed for the ultimate disaster.

But if The Fool belongs here, at the end, then perhaps this figure is not, after all, such a fool as he seems. It may simply be that you must make a blind leap of faith to achieve the final step in your path to enlightenment, frightening though it may be. And though it may appear to the observer that you are walking blindly toward your doom, perhaps what you are really heading for is a transformation so far outside the limits of this world that it cannot be imagined even by the most accomplished adept.

I leave it to you to decide for yourself if The Fool is simply someone too stupid to watch where he's going, and who is therefore headed for disaster. Or if he is someone whose faith is so great that he is willing to take a major step without questioning where it may lead him. Either way, he's walking blindly to his fate. Arcanum Zero asks if you would—or could—do the same.

In the Reading

Upright (or Positive): Folly, thoughtlessness, extravagance, lack of discipline, delirium, frenzy.

Reversed (or Negative): Carelessness, negligence, apathy. Hesitation, instability.

If this card describes a situation, then you are being told that it would be foolish to get involved in that situation, or spend any effort resolving it. If it describes or is near a person, then that individual is a fool, or involved in some foolish enterprise.

If this card represents the querent, then just ahead of you lies a choice of the greatest importance to you and your future. If you continue in the way you've been going, your greatest possibility is almost certain destruction. If you pay attention to the warning signs, there is still a chance that you can avoid this disaster.

In effect, however, if this card comes up, you are being told to watch your step, to use your head, to stop being a deliberate idiot.

[Note: In most cases, the querent for whom The Fool comes up in a reading knows very well that he or she is being foolish, but is refusing to acknowledge it because they just don't want to see it.]

Notes

MORE ON THE MAJOR ARCANA

There is even more that you can learn from and accomplish with the Major Arcana than I've covered here, or that can be covered in a book of this nature. Before moving on, however, let's take at least a brief look at one of the ways you can make practical use of these cards.

Spiritual progress is important, but you have to live in this world, too. As you may have already concluded on your own by this point, it is possible to use the Major Arcana for temporal personal progress as well as spiritual. To accomplish this, you need to select the appropriate card for your purpose. Then you use its imagery to create changes in yourself that will enable you to cope better and function more effectively in your day-to-day life.

This is also a meditation use of the Tarot, but one in which you use the cards of the Major Arcana to help you reach a single, specific goal. For example: Strength (Arcanum Eleven) is a card of endurance and triumph against opposition. Its function is to enable you to defeat not only enemies outside your Self, but the enemies within, to overcome your own base passions and flaws.

Now let's say you have a habit or behavior pattern that you haven't been able to change, no matter how hard you tried. Your problem may be a character trait, such as extreme shyness, or it may be an addiction, as to smoking, or overeating. Using whatever meditation technique works for you, focus your attention on the imagery of the Strength card. Place *your* image of your-self (i.e., whatever shape or picture best illustrates the way you see yourself) in the position of the figure who is fighting—and overcoming!—the lion. Then create a visual image of your habit or trait, and put it in the picture in place of the lion. See yourself bending this problem to your will and finally breaking or defeating it. When you know that you are the master of this particular passion, you will be.

If that doesn't work for you, try a different card. Every person and every situation is different, and there are a variety of approaches available to you through the Major Arcana. For example, let's say that the real reason you haven't eliminated a particular habit, such as smoking, is not because you can't, but because you don't really want to. Yet you do recognize that you would be better off without this habit. If that is the situation you're in, you don't have an enemy to overcome. But there is something you have to give up in order to attain a greater good, such as better health. The Hanged Man (Arcanum Twelve), with its symbolism of sacrifice for the purpose of attaining a greater goal, might serve your purpose better.

However, whether or not you can use a particular card also depends on whether or not you can put yourself in that picture. If visualizing yourself in a given situation makes you uncomfortable, then no matter how appropriate the card for your purpose, you can't use it.

In such a case, it is completely legitimate to bypass even a card which specifically states your problem, and select another one whose imagery is less threatening and/or more personally satisfying. For example, The World (Arcanum Twenty-One) could also be used to help break a habit or change a character trait, in this case as a picture of the end result—your success and feelings of total attainment—rather than the process of working toward it. Or you may want to visualize yourself as The Magician (Arcanum One), easily and confidently manipulating your trait or habit and thereby bending it to your will.

So the criteria for selecting the right card for your purpose depends on three factors: what imagery you can relate to best in these circumstances; a clear understanding of the goal you want to reach; and an even clearer understanding of exactly where you're starting from and why.

Note that even with the right card for the right job, none of these changes in your basic Self will take place overnight. What you're doing is altering your mindset; literally making yourself over from the person you were into the kind of person you would rather be. How long it will take you to succeed in your effort depends on the nature of the situation, on your meditation technique and how well you use it, and on how long it takes you to learn this technique. But the change will come more easily, and be more lasting, with the help of the Tarot.

And each change you make in your own psyche will be easier than the one before. As you learn more about the Tarot, and more about yourself as a result, you'll eventually begin to almost instinctively choose the card you need, and employ the best way to use it.

In the meantime, experiment. We can all use a little help in reaching—and sometimes even in identifying—our personal goals and needs.

The Tarot, more than any other tool, gives you an effective means to control, improve, direct, and even re-create the most important element in your world—yourself. There are unquestionably situations where forces outside your personal control are responsible for your problems. But in more cases than not, a change in yourself can work an almost miraculous change in your environment.

The Magician stands at the center of the universe and all things radiate out from there. You are the center of your universe: the focal point. Change the focus, and everything else will follow.

Now let's take a look at the other deck of the Tarot: the Minor Arcana.

The Minor Arcana

The Minor Arcana

INTRODUCTION

The Minor, or Lesser, Arcana of the Tarot deck consists of fifty-six cards. These are divided into four suits of fourteen cards each: Swords, Cups, Coins (also called Deniers or Pentacles), and Wands (also called Batons, or Clubs, the name by which they are known in modern playing decks).

Each suit is further divided into number (or pip) cards, and face cards (or court cards). There are ten pip cards (Ace through Ten) and four court cards (King, Queen, Knight, and Page) per suit.

As we discussed earlier, it is the cards of the Minor Arcana that were eventually transformed into our modern deck of playing cards. The relative "strength" of each suit has also carried over into at least some of today's card games. In the game of Bridge, for example, the rank of suits is Spades, Hearts, Diamonds, and Clubs. This is the same order of precedence they follow in the Tarot: Swords, Cups, Coins, and Wands, respectively.

Many books on the Tarot pay very little attention to the Minor Arcana. Usually you will get no more than a brief list of meanings for each of the cards. And even these sketchy definitions vary widely from book to book.

Part of the problem in establishing definitive interpretations may exist because in most decks these cards do not have anything like the storytelling illustrations of the Major Arcana. The pip cards simply display the corresponding number of their suit symbol; the arrangement is usually symmetrical, but basically arbitrary, and does not reflect the interpretation of the cards. What's more, the intrinsic design of the suit symbols varies from deck to deck, and often within a single deck as well.

The court cards also lack any real clues as to the character of the individuals depicted. These are not illuminated drawings; the people in them are not shown performing any distinctive activity, nor do they have any symbolic props or distinctive background art. They are simply straightforward pictures of a King, a Queen, a Knight and a Page. While there may be some variations in costume, the only real way to tell one suit from another is that each court card is labeled at the bottom, and each of the four individuals named is shown with the symbol of their suit.

At least one exception to this is Waite's deck, where the pip cards do show some kind of activity involving each suit's symbols, though the court cards are still fairly standard. Even Waite admits, however, that these illustrations are somewhat apocryphal. There was a time when all the cards of the Tarot were decorated with illustrations, but it was evidently just a way of making the decks more attractive. The illustrations were largely the inventions of individual artists, and did not explain (and in some cases flatly contradicted) the divinatory meanings of the cards.

So whether or not a deck is illuminated, there are few, if any, traditional elements in the design of the Minor Arcana. Many generations of many Tarot adepts working with these cards have produced some agreement on their interpretation, but they have also produced a great deal of disagreement as well. Also, without a standard to refer to, such as exists for the Major Arcana, it can be very difficult to determine exactly what these cards are meant to reveal.

There is also the possibility that the reason there is no definitive art is because there were no definitive meanings for the Minor Arcana to begin with. These cards are not, after all, a record of ancient magical teachings. In fact, not only did they evolve into common playing cards, but they probably started out that way as well! And while they do make an extremely accurate divining tool when read correctly, the number of contradictory interpretations sometimes makes it seem as though it's up to each reader to decide what the cards really mean.

Whatever the reason for the difficulty, there is a lot of disagreement as to just how these cards should be interpreted, and even what they are doing in the Tarot deck at all.

Understanding the Minor Arcana

Most research evidence points to the probability that the Minor Arcana of the Tarot is in fact a second, separate deck, which was appended to the Major Arcana sometime in the fourteenth or fifteenth centuries. The way these cards are usually interpreted supports this theory. There is generally no reference to arcane learning or spiritual growth. Instead, interpretations focus on this world and recount mundane situations and events.

Throughout the centuries, attempts have been made to find some higher philosophical meaning in the Minor Arcana, probably because of the obvious spiritual significance of the Major Arcana. But these cards are simply not a meditation device. Within the context of the Tarot, there is little reason to suppose that the Minor Arcana is, or ever was, anything but a fortunetelling tool.

None of this means, however, that the Minor Arcana has no real significance. If you understand the reason for the incorporation of these cards into the Tarot deck, you'll realize that it's not necessary to try to find or invent some mystical meaning for them. Their own meaning is valid enough.

The function of the Minor Arcana is to describe the everyday world. It provides both an historical and cultural background to the individual's struggle to come to terms with his or her inner reality. In effect, while the Major Arcana explores the soul, the Minor Arcana places the individual within the context of society.

Since it is in our interactions with the outside world that we need to know what will happen, it is appropriate to include in the Tarot a way to discover just what that world has in store for us. It is this combination—a picture of personal striving set against a background of actual events—which makes the Tarot the accurate and specific divination tool that it is.

The Major Arcana is built on the premise that each individual is a microcosm: an entire universe contained within one self-aware being. But there is also a macrocosm—a larger and often indifferent universe—within which each of us lives and moves. And no matter what steps you may take to improve yourself, or to build on your own personal potential, everything you try to do is inevitably going to be influenced by that larger world of which you are only one part. It is the Minor Arcana which reveals and describes just what that larger world is up to at any given time, and exactly how that will affect you.

The lessons of the Minor Arcana, therefore, are no less important than those of the Major Arcana. It teaches that no event happens in a vacuum, everything follows from something else. The more sincere a seeker after truth you are, the more you need this lesson, because it is a fact that people who focus on the magickal and the mystical often tend to overlook or even forget that there is a real world out there that has to be dealt with at the same time. By combining within itself the mystical and the mundane, the Tarot reinforces the lesson that though you may be striving for the other world, you still have to live in this one.

How to Begin Your Interpretation of the Minor Arcana

The four suits of the Minor Arcana originally represented the four main classes of people in medieval society. With very slight adjustments, they can be understood as they correspond to modern society as well. Times may change and technology may advance, but people stay pretty much the same.

Swords represented the nobility, with all their absolute temporal power, their ability (and tendency!) to wage war and to control, often capriciously, the lives and deaths of all other classes. In the reading, Swords have come to represent the power and forces of hatred and violence. These cards describe your enemies, whether individuals, organized groups, or impersonal forces; anyone or anything that wants to harm you, or to control you for their own ends.

Cups represented the clergy, the second most influential class in medieval society. It refers primarily to the local priests, who did what they could to alleviate at least some of the evils that afflicted their parishioners. The suit of Cups has come to represent the power of love and faith. The presence of these cards in a reading indicates that there are individuals, groups, or forces who will work in your favor for no other reason than that they care about you.

Coins represented the merchant class. Neither nobility nor serfs, the merchants bought and sold, opened trade routes, provided financing for many ventures, and made a lot of money for themselves. They controlled the power of money, and this suit represents the influence, for good or bad, of material wealth in your life.

Lowest on the social scale was the peasant or serf class, represented by Wands. Virtual slaves, serfs had little hope of improving their position in life, except by joining the church or successfully running away; either of which rarely happened. Wands in a reading describes the ability or potential to succeed despite tremendous odds.

Basically, then, the Minor Arcana divides the mundane world into four main categories: forces that work against you, forces that work for you, the influence of material possessions, and the ability and determination to succeed. On the surface, this may seem an oversimplification. There is more to the physical universe, after all, than hate, love, money, and ambition.

But these four elements are the basis of any social grouping, simple or complex. Therefore, these are the forces that directly affect you, either because they are directed at you, or directed by you. Like the Major Arcana, it is the individual with whom the Minor Arcana is primarily concerned. While you're pursuing your own personal goals, says the Minor Arcana, these are the factors in your social environment that will either aid or impede you.

The four suits of the Minor Arcana also correspond to the four elements. Here the historical connection reaches back to the rituals of the ancient Druids: Sword of Fire, Cup of Water, Dish of Earth, and Spear or Wand of Air. It is partly because of this more ancient association that Tarot scholars feel that the Minor Arcana must be older than it appears.

Within each suit, the relationships of the cards are similar. The pip cards describe events or situations. These events progress in a logical and coherent order: each one results from the ones before and causes those which follow.

The court cards sometimes describe situations as well. But they can also describe specific people who will influence the outcome of a series of events.

When the court cards represent situations, they give the reading its "story line": i.e., they explain the nature of the state of affairs in which the querent, the person for whom the reading is done, is involved. For example, if court cards from the suit of Cups appear in the reading, then the querent's emotional reactions to people or events, or the feelings of other people toward the querent, will have the greatest effect on the outcome of the situation. The higher the rank of the court card, the more influence this state of affairs will have on the querent's judgement, and/or ability to resolve the situation.

When the court cards represent people, then those people possess some or all of the characteristics of their suit. But they also possess an operating intelligence which deliberately puts those characteristics into play. In all cases, therefore, cards which represent people have a much stronger influence on the reading than cards which describe situations or events.

The reason is easy to understand. If a given situation is simply happenstance, some other happenstance can negate it. But if an intelligent individual is deliberately planning or causing a situation, it will take at least an equal and opposite intelligence to change it. So when the court cards signal the active interest of other people in your life, whatever they're planning, for good or bad, must be taken into careful consideration by the reader.

The Tarot's Royal Court

The court cards are named King, Queen, Knight (or Cavalier), and Page (or Valet). These designations should be understood as a literal description of the type of authority each of these personages has within their own domain (or their own suit).

A King is a powerful man who exercises absolute control over the territory he rules. Even if there are other powerful people within that same territory, the King outclasses them all. He has greater authority than anyone else in the same domain; he holds the highest position; he is acknowledged as ruler even by his competitors. In the Minor Arcana, the King of any suit is the ruler of that suit: a powerful man who not only possesses all the knowledge, abilities, and characteristics of his suit, but who has those attributes to a superior degree. He also has the necessary authority to make things happen the way he chooses.

The Queen is the female counterpart of the King. She also personifies the characteristics of her suit and has an absolute monarch's power over her subjects. Where the King of the same suit is present, she is his consort; that is she takes the wife's role, supporting and strengthening the King's actions and decisions. Where there is no King in a given domain (in this case, in a reading), she rules in her own right.

In most older interpretations of the Tarot, the same qualities which, in the King, are considered virtues or strengths became vices or weaknesses in the Queen. This tendency to resent strengths in a woman that are admired in a man exists even in our own time, but it is not an accurate interpretation.

The Queen of any suit has exactly the same strengths and weaknesses as the King of the same suit. While she does possess and use a feminine perspective which contrasts and complements the King's masculine approach, her power and authority are equal to those of her consort. She should be understood as a woman who embodies within herself all the qualities of a born ruler.

A Knight is a man who has been elevated to that position by his monarch because of services he performed which benefit the crown. Once knighted, he is expected to continue to render those services. In the Tarot, the Knight is not only a loyal subject of the crown, he is also the allegorical son of the King and Queen. This card, therefore, depicts a young man who possesses qualities and characteristics similar to those of his royal parents.

The Knight has these qualities to a lesser degree, however. He certainly lacks the absolute authority of the King and Queen, and in many ways, he lacks their maturity as well. Because of the Knight's lesser ability and experience, he can sometimes be either more dangerous or less effective, depending on the suit, than his royal parents.

He should not be underestimate, however. He does have the potential to become what the King and Queen now are, and he has every good reason to believe in and fight for the prerogatives and position of his house. He is, after all, the heir apparent; anything that forwards the goals and purposes of his allegorical parents also serves his own ends.

Because the Knight is usually depicted as wearing armor and riding a horse, this card also carries several additional interpretations, either relating to the character of the Knight, or (if the card does not represent a person) describing current or upcoming situations. The Knight may be seen as a warrior (specifically one prepared to do battle on behalf of his house); or the card may indicate that there is or will be some kind of conflict. The Knight may also be a messenger or go-between; or the card may indicate messages sent or received. It can also be interpreted as having to do with travel, change of scene, or movement from one place, or one type of situation, to another. Which of these interpretations apply will usually be made clear by the other cards in the reading.

Note also that in modern readings, it has sometimes happened that the Knight card represents a young woman rather than a young man. If so, she has the exact same qualities as described here.

A Page is the personal attendant of the royal family. In a medieval monarchy, this young servitor held a higher position in the household than merely hired help. The page was generally a younger son or daughter who was serving an apprenticeship: in the process of waiting on parents or older siblings, he or she was also being taught proper behavior and the ins and outs of the family business.

This is the case in the Tarot. The Page is a younger child of the King and Queen and has the same characteristics as other family members, though again, to a lesser degree. This card may represent either a male or female; he or she will be someone younger or less experienced than the Knight. The Page also often has many of the characteristics of a child, or exhibits a child's behavior. He or she is very proud of being part of the royal family; and this pride, depending on the suit, may result in either endearing characteristics or the obnoxious behavior of a spoiled brat. Either way, this is still someone who wants to see the purposes of their house (their suit) succeed.

Taken together, the court cards constitute a royal family. Their relationship to the querent is that of family members, or of people who have the status of family members in the querent's life. This gives them additional authority, over and above their own personal ability to control events, because, in this situation at least, they also have a very strong personal influence on the querent.

The King and Queen, for example, are parental figures. They may be either your actual parents, or someone who stands *in loco parentis*—such as an employer, a teacher, an advisor, even a police officer, any person you respect, fear, and/or are likely to obey, especially in the situation covered by the reading. Given the social position of the King and Queen, the person represented by these cards may actually have even greater authority than a parent, or than your parent usually does, at least in these circumstances.

Whoever they are, they will always be mature individuals. They must be old enough to be firmly established in their positions of authority and influence; they are also old enough to have full-grown children. This would put them, at the very least, in their forties or early fifties, and possibly older.

The Knight is also an adult, but one generation younger than the King or Queen; his age range is anywhere from late twenties up to early or mid-thirties. As far as social position is concerned, the card represents a young man (or woman) who has reason to believe, rightly or wrongly, that he is next in line for the throne. He may be the actual son of a powerful individual, or he may be the heir apparent in some other way. For example, in a reading having to do with finance, the Knight could be a rising young executive in a company with which the querent must do business in this situation.

Whether or not the Knight is actually related to the King or Queen, he is someone they will listen to—because they can trust him to understand their goals and help them accomplish their purposes. This means that, in addition to any abilities or influence of his own, he can also act as an intercessor for the querent, to get the attention or favor of the rulers of his house. Or, if the reading shows him in opposition to the querent, he may be someone who will deliberately use his influence against you.

The Page has some influence as well, but generally much less than he or she thinks they do. This is someone who can be helpful, or spiteful and malicious in a petty way, but who does not have even the degree of authority possessed by the Knight. If we use the example of the Knight as a rising young executive, the Page would be in an entry-level position in the same company. He or she may be someone whose potential and loyalty is recognized, and who may be given important duties to perform, but who is unlikely to be consulted, or even told, when there are important decisions to be made.

Most of this has to do with youth and inexperience. The Page may be either a young child, or a half-grown one, but will rarely, if ever, be older than late teens or early 20s. As a result, even if the Page is related to, and indulged by, the King or Queen, this person's opinions and advice are not always taken seriously by other members of the royal family.

Nonetheless, the Page should be taken seriously by the querent. He or she may not be the top gun, but this is still someone whose friendship can benefit and enmity can hurt you.

The relationship of each of these people to the querent would depend, then, on the querent's own age and social position. If the querent is fairly young (less than thirty), then either the King or Queen would be someone old enough to be their parents. If the querent is old enough to have grown children, then either the Knight or the Page could represent their child, or someone young enough to be their child. If the querent is in the same age range as a person represented by a court card, then obviously that individual is someone in their own generation; or the card may represent the querent.

Bear in mind, however, that since the court cards may not represent actual family members, age relative to the querent is not always a determining factor in establishing exact relationships. The King, for example, is a father figure, but if the querent is mature, then the actual person the King represents may not be old enough to be the querent's father. What he will be is someone in a position to exercise a father's authority or influence over the querent.

A number of sources on the Tarot also give general physical descriptions for the members of the four royal families as an aid to establishing their exact identities. But while telling someone that they are soon to meet a tall, dark stranger can be impressive, it's been found that an attempt to give specific physical descriptions can sometimes be more misleading than helpful in determining just who these cards represent.

For example, people in the Swords suit are usually described as being dark in coloring; people from the Cups suit are usually described as fair. But in real life, the good guy doesn't always wear a white hat, nor does the bad guy always have a black mustache. Physical descriptions of the people in the court cards are more useful as a guideline for choosing a card to represent the querent, or identifying one that does. Otherwise, it's more accurate to consider this "coloring" to be a description of character or personality, rather than actual physical appearance. In most cases, age, social position, and character traits are all the information you need to give you a clue to the identity of these individuals.

When these cards appear in a reading, then, your first task is to determine whether they represent people or situations, and if they represent people, to find out who they are in real life. How easy or difficult either task will be depends on the circumstances of the reading. If the card represents a person the querent has already met (i.e.: if the card appears as an influence in the querent's past or present), then once you've described that person's character and influence on the situation, the querent will usually be able to identify them. If, after you've given all possible descriptions, no one in the querent's life resembles that person, then the court card describes a situation.

When the card appears as a future influence, you'll just have to wait to find out who or what it represents. If it's a person, the querent will recognize them when he or she meets them. If it's a situation, then when it starts to happen, at least the querent will know just what they're getting into.

How to Use This Guide

Since the Minor Arcana is primarily a fortunetelling tool, the focus in the following section is on what these cards mean in a reading.

There are five chapters in this part of the book. The first chapter (Interpreting the Minor Arcana) is a general guide to understanding and reading the cards. It includes a brief explanation of how the interpretations given for each card were selected, and how to use them in a reading. There is also a detailed description of an alternate method which you can use for interpreting the cards. And finally, there is an overview of the advantages and disadvantages of different types of decks.

The next four chapters cover the suits of the Minor Arcana in detail. As with the section on the Major Arcana, all four suits are described according to the same system. First, there is an explanation of the cultural and personal experiences the suit represents, beginning with its historical background and then giving its application to modern times.

Next there is a brief description of the various ways the suit symbols are drawn, and the symbolic meanings of those designs.

Finally, there is a card by card listing for each suit. First the court cards are described, beginning with the King, then the pip cards, beginning with the Ace. For every card, two separate but corresponding interpretations are given. The first ("Meaning") gives you the basic interpretation of the card, explaining what it means independently of any reading. For the court cards only, this explanation includes a description of the kind of person each card portrays; for both court and pip cards, the general situation the card reveals is also outlined. The second section ("In the Reading") is a list of the various interpretations each card has in a Tarot layout.

Because there are no standard illustrations for the Minor Arcana, no great attempt has been made to describe the cards. I have included a general description of each of the court cards. This is primarily a way to help you distinguish the cards of each suit, and especially to differentiate them from any cards in the Major Arcana which may be slightly similar (for example: the King and Queen court cards often resemble the Emperor and Empress in some respects). As explained above, however, there is usually no symbolic significance in the portrayal of the Tarot's royal courts.

For the pip cards, only the Ace is described; the arrangement of symbols on the remaining cards, and any decorations that may be included, are usually the invention of the artist who designed the deck, and, again, have no mystical significance. Because of the lack of a standard which does have mystical significance, I have not included in these chapters a description of any illuminated deck.

As you read through each of these chapters, examine the cards in your deck, just to familiarize yourself with them. Don't expect or try to memorize the interpretations all at once. You'll learn to use them with practice, and over time. Until you do, these chapters are arranged so that you can use them as a reference while you do your first Tarot readings.

Minor Arcana

INTERPRETATION

When you begin to do your own research on the Minor Arcana, you'll find a curious mix of agreement and disagreement on the meaning of these cards. Some expert readers have their own unique interpretations; others seem to echo what everyone else says. Sometimes, two separate sources which disagree on the meaning of one card will agree on the interpretation of another. Even if you use only one source, however, it still seems as though you can't get a straight answer about how to interpret the cards, because in most cases all you do get is simply a long list of disconnected words and phrases for each card, with no explanation of how to apply them to any given reading.

Time and experience will teach you which definitions, from the many sources available, best describe the meaning of any given card. As you work with the Tarot, you will also learn how to decide, given a list of workable definitions, which one applies to a specific reading, and how it should be interpreted in that situation. None of this is helpful, however, if you've never read Tarot before. You need a place to start making your own determinations of what the cards are trying to tell you.

Getting Started

Since this is a beginner's text, it would not be helpful to simply give you yet another list of interpretations, without at least some reference to what you'll find in other sources. What I've done, therefore, is to survey a number of sources on the Tarot, both texts and expert readers, to find out where they agree and where they don't. After some consultation (and not a little bit of argument), I selected those interpretations on which most of my sources agree, eliminating any definitions which vary widely (though they, too, may possibly have been accurate in some circumstances).

I have not, of course, included all sources on the Tarot in this research. But the list of meanings provided for each card does give you a kind of summary of those definitions which many readers and researchers of the Tarot (including myself) have found to be accurate and workable. You'll find this list of definitions under the heading "In the Reading" for each card.

But that still leaves you with just a long list of words and phrases. How do you make a choice as to which definition applies in a given reading? How do you even know what these definitions are intended to mean in the first place?

For the Major Arcana, you at least have a sound understanding of what each card means in its own right. That's enough to help you adjust the divinatory meanings to suit a given situation.

For the Minor Arcana, all you have is a general description of each suit as a whole. If you could get an idea of exactly what kind of event or situation each card describes, it would be easier to determine what part of it applies to a reading you're doing.

So along with the list of definitions, you'll also find a general interpretation of each card, under the heading "Meaning." This interpretation explains the nature of the situation which the presence of that card in a reading reveals. For the court cards, it also includes a description of the kind of person you're dealing with. When you begin doing readings, you can use either the list of definitions, or this overall interpretation, or both, as a guide to understanding the message each card is trying to reveal.

Even with all these explanations, learning to read the Minor Arcana isn't easy. Because the cards offer so few visual cues, it can often be difficult for beginning readers (and even some experienced ones!) to remember their meanings.

But there is a way to understand and remember the various interpretations, and adjust them accurately, without waiting until you have years of experience behind you to give you an expert reader's instinctive understanding of the cards.

As with the Major Arcana, there is a correspondence between the Minor Arcana and the general precepts of numerology. Even more than for the Major Arcana, the definitions of the numbers clarify and agree with the most commonly accepted interpretations of these cards.

Numerological correspondences can be used to interpret cards of the same rank, independently of their suit. Because they are the same for each suit, they serve as a useful mnemonic for remembering the basic meanings of the cards. They also provide a means for adjusting the interpretations as the necessities of any reading demands. This method of interpreting the Minor Arcana has proven, over time, to be an accurate system for determining a working meaning of the cards.

By the Numbers

You don't have to know a lot about numerology to use it as a guide to interpreting the pip cards of the Minor Arcana. All you need are the cyclical meanings of the numbers. This will give you, for each card, a picture of the events taking place or the situation which is currently in the process of playing itself out. It will also tell you what stage of the game you're at, how far along this series of events has progressed, and, therefore, how deeply involved the querent is at this point in time.

The suit of the card will tell you the nature of the situation: what kind of forces, attitudes, or needs are controlling or defining this series of events. Add the two together, and you have a workable interpretation of the card.

ONE is the number of beginnings, of original action, or of creativity. If the Ace in your reading is upright, or the reading is generally favorable, then the beginning in question will be auspicious. If the card is reversed (or the reading unfavorable), then the series of events now beginning—or their results, if nothing is done about it—will be unfortunate.

TWO is the number of union, imagination, and conception. In a reading, the deuce indicates that some new factor is about to be introduced into the current situation—another person, an event, a circumstance—

which will have a profound impact on the course of events. If the indications are favorable, that new factor will be of benefit to you. It will help you reach a desired outcome or avoid an unwanted one. If the indications are unfavorable, then that new factor will work against you. It will make difficult or prevent the accomplishment of a desired goal, or increase the chances of an undesirable outcome.

THREE is the number of expression, or self-expression. It is also the response to, or outcome of, events in one and two: new beginnings, plus union or conception. It is at this point that some situation which you've recently initiated or gotten involved in will begin to take on a form and direction of its own. If the reading is unfavorable, then this is when everything is going to start turning sour; even if things originally started off well, they're going downhill from here. If the reading is favorable, then you're off to a running start. Even if things started out badly, they are now more likely to bear positive fruit.

FOUR is a number of hard work, and careful planning. By this time, you have a basic understanding of the situation you're in. Now is when you have to work effectively to make it all come out as you want it to. If you like the situation you're in, you have to work and plan to make it continue to grow; if you don't, then now is when you have to work and plan to end or alleviate it. But FOUR is also a number of unconventional behavior and sudden, unexpected events. You must also be aware that some new factor can suddenly enter into the situation which will change everything for better or worse—no matter how hard you work and plan. The position of this card in the reading, and of surrounding cards, will tell you whether it's better or worse that you can expect.

FIVE is the number of movement, excitement, and adventure. While this may seem to be an advantageous indicator, never forget there is also an old curse which states: "May you live in interesting times." People who get drafted into the military during a war also have excitement and adventure, but it is unquestionably of a type they could do without! If a FIVE card adds favorable indications to a reading, then your plans are moving toward a particularly exciting result, and/or you can expect to really enjoy upcoming situations and events. If unfavorable, then you can expect upheaval and disorder, and even ruin of everything you've worked for.

SIX is the number of harmony, of balance and adjustment, of quiet circumstances and activities. It is also the number of love and romance. In a favorable reading, it means you can expect a bit of peace after all the activity and excitement. Misunderstandings can or will be cleared up at this time, either between people or within your own mind. In effect, you have a chance to stop and catch your breath. You made your plans, you took your chances; now you can tie it all together in a coherent state. If the card or reading is unfavorable, however, there are still some rocky shoals ahead. Fortunately, SIX indicators are never as unfavorable as other cards. But the circumstances you face can still, nonetheless, be very uncomfortable.

SEVEN is the number of solitude, and of soul-searching. This need not necessarily be on the spiritual level; you can search your soul with psychoanalysis, too! However, it indicates a period when you'll find it necessary to seriously consider how and why specific events come to pass. If the reading is favorable, that course of events could be almost miraculous, and you may have occasion to wonder how it is that all of a sudden things worked out so well. If unfavorable, then the possibility is strong that you're deluding yourself, making bad decisions, and getting into deep waters. In any case, you are in a position where you're literally taking a flyer on faith. It's necessary to be certain that your faith—in others, in events, or even in yourself—is justified.

EIGHT is the number of energy and efficiency, of using wisdom learned through experience. It is also a number of caution, self-discipline, and personal security (financial and otherwise). If the reading is favorable, then whatever your goal, go for it; this is your time to get ahead in the world, and you should grasp the opportunity with both hands. If the card or the reading is unfavorable, then those same responsibilities and challenges will be a burden, bringing unhappiness, perhaps even despair.

NINE is the number of completeness. The series of events has reached or is reaching its inevitable outcome, for good or bad, and everything is about to be made clear. NINE is also a number of originality and initiative, but with them the contradictory traits of vulnerability and naivete. If the reading is favorable, then even though things have reached their conclusion, there is still time to take some further action, if necessary, to salvage something from the ruins of a bad situation. If the reading is unfavorable, then even though you've completed the task, done everything you should or could do, the possibility exists that there was something vital you overlooked, and/or that someone or something is going to step in at the last minute and bring everything down in ruins.

TEN is both an end and a beginning. It's an end because, for good or bad, the situation you've been involved in for so long is now complete. It's time to move on. This is especially good advice if you're particularly satisfied with your current circumstances; people do have a tendency to rest on their laurels. It's also something you need to know if the series of events up to this point has been personally devastating. At least now it's all over.

It's a beginning because life itself is cyclical, a never-ending saga, and everything that we experience along the way changes us to a greater or lesser extent. The person who initiates or gets involved in the next series of events will not be the same person who just completed this one.

As a compound number, TEN has a greater impact than ONE. It's a number of rise and fall, of good and evil, of extreme responses like love or hate, pride or fear. It allows no middle ground. If the reading is favorable, then you know that you can go on from here in security and honor. If unfavorable, then any gains will be illusionary and the next series of events coming up will be adversely affected as well.

When the court cards represent people, then you interpret their influence on the reading based on the characteristics of those people. If they represent situations or events, then they can also be read by the numbers. Here again, you'll find that the numerological interpretations match the characteristics of either the people or events these cards ordinarily describe. As with the TEN, however, these are compound numbers; so their influence on the reading has an added dimension.

ELEVEN (The Page): As the compound of TWO, this is a number of conflict and opposition, even of treachery. It may indicate two people whose goals conflict, or two opposed situations. If the reading is favorable, the conflict can be resolved, either on your own initiative, or with help from a friend or relative. If unfavorable, then you're in for a lot of worry and complications. Expect bad news.

TWELVE (The Knight): This is a number of sacrifice. Either you'll be asked to give up something that matters to you, or perhaps a friend or relative will perform an unselfish act on your behalf. But there are plans and intrigues going on in the background of which you may or may not be aware, and in which you are about to become involved—whether you want to or not. If the reading is favorable, you'll learn something positive or benefit in some other way from all this. If unfavorable, then the people involved are working for their own ends, and the possibility exists that you're being used. In either case, it's necessary to be alert to the real situation. People who are actually working for you may appear to be enemies; people who are actually enemies may pretend to be on your side. Be alert and be cautious; and beware of false flattery from those who use it to gain their own ends. Forewarned is forearmed.

THIRTEEN (The Queen): As before, this is not an intrinsically unlucky number. And while it is the number of upheaval, that upheaval exists so that new ground can be broken. THIRTEEN is a number of regeneration and change. But it's also a very powerful number, and you are well advised to walk carefully; if the power is used selfishly, it can bring its own destruction. In a favorable reading, bad is being swept away to allow good to come in. In an unfavorable reading, destruction is the result, with malicious forces working against you. Upheaval even for a good end is still uncomfortable, but if you can at least see where it's going you can live with it. But if your world is about to be turned upside down just for spite, you have to gather all your forces to fight back.

FOURTEEN (The King): This is a number of challenges and change. It is also a number of luck. Both gains and losses can be temporary, because of the continual change; you will also be challenged to your full extent. Be cautious in dealings with those in authority; they may be for you or against you, but they have their own agendas to deal with first. The challenge here is that you should rely on yourself, rather than depending on the word or assistance of others. The "luck" of FOURTEEN includes money dealings and speculative projects (like betting), but there's always a danger of loss due to wrong advice from others, or misplaced overconfidence. If this card adds favorable indicators to a reading, then you will meet the challenges ahead and succeed; and, in the process, become stronger and more self-reliant. If unfavorable, you will either let yourself be used, or fail in your efforts; either way, you face almost certain defeat.

If you do learn to read the Minor Arcana "by the numbers," it will give you an additional divinatory tool as well. Should you find yourself without your Tarot deck, you can use any ordinary deck of playing cards to foretell upcoming events. Your forecasts will not be as detailed, because you'll lack both the input from the Major Arcana and four cards from the Minor Arcana (the four Knights); but they will be accurate.

When you use a regular deck, all you have to do is drop the last compound number: the Jack is eleven, the Queen is twelve, and the King is thirteen. For the suit meanings, substitute Spades for Swords, Hearts for Cups, Diamonds for Coins, and Clubs for Wands.

On a personal note: don't do it too often. It's a lot of fun, and it can be very impressive to tell accurate fortunes with an ordinary deck. But there are disadvantages as well. Teach yourself to automatically recognize the messages in an regular deck of playing cards, and it can really spoil a friendly game!

Choosing Your Deck

Whether you use a standard deck or one in which the pip cards are illuminated must be your choice. There are advantages and disadvantages to both deck designs.

For some Tarot readers, illustrations on the pip cards of the Minor Arcana can clarify the meaning of the cards, or at the very least act as a mnemonic to help you remember their meaning. But they can also be confusing, since sometimes the interpretation of a card seems to contradict whatever is going on in the picture.

On the other hand, the standard decks offer no clues at all, contradictory or otherwise. In most cases, only the court cards even have an obvious upright and reverse. And while the pip cards are usually numbered, there are decks in which these labels are left off as well. It can sometimes seem as though the Tarot is going out of its way to make the Minor Arcana even more of a mystery than the Major Arcana.

But the lack of visual cues can actually be an advantage. If you use a standard deck, the static representations on the pip cards allow you to evoke your own images, different for each reading, of what is going on in the situation being described. People do react very strongly to pictures. (As you'll find when you start doing readings. The illustrations on the Major Arcana distract and even upset those querents who don't understand their symbolism.) There also are Tarot readers who find illustrations on the pip cards distracting as well.

For those readers who prefer a standard deck, the primary disadvantage is the lack of a definable upright or reverse for most of the cards. If you're more comfortable using upright and reverse in your readings, however, there are ways to get around that problem. You can use a deck where the pip cards are not designed symmetrically, so that you can tell top from bottom. Or, you can arbitrarily establish a top and bottom on your cards by simply marking one side.

If you find a deck where the Minor Arcana is illuminated, and you're comfortable with the symbolism, by all means use that deck. Keep in mind, however, that these pictures should not necessarily be taken at face value. Be sure you choose a deck where the pictures illustrate *your* interpretation of the cards (or, at least, don't contradict it).

And never forget that the Minor Arcana is not a meditation tool. Illustrations on illuminated decks are not derived, insofar as is known, from any ancient mystical knowledge; the symbolism employed is generally the invention of each deck's designer. Don't let the illustrations interfere with your ability to understand and interpret the divinatory meanings of the cards.

Reading the Cards

No matter what kind of deck you use, or interpretation system you follow, you have to learn the meanings of the cards in order to do a reading. But there is one very important thing you don't have to learn.

The Minor Arcana describes social conditions and events. You don't need any kind of special training, or any scholarly or mystical background, to understand those situations. This is *your* culture that is being described, after all; you grew up in it, you live with it every day of your life. And so you know what a given social situation is like; you can easily visualize the circumstances described in a reading.

The only element in a reading that is not part of your personal experience is the nature and reactions of the querent. Should you need to know that to understand a specific situation, the cards of the Major Arcana will tell you what kind of person you're dealing with. (In fact, even if you do a reading for yourself, which is one of the hardest to do, you should follow what the Major Arcana tells you about the "querent.")

For everything else, you have the knowledge that you need to interpret the information the cards will give you. Don't be afraid to make your own adjustments as you learn more about Tarot applications! Your own insights are the most valuable tool you have in interpreting the Tarot.

Swords

THE SUIT OF SWORDS

Of all four suits, Swords is the most powerful—and the most dangerous. It represents true worldly power, but power which is often misused and abused for selfish purposes. In a reading, Swords warns of enemies, danger, misfortune, even violence and death.

Originally the suit of the nobility, or warrior class, Swords allegorizes the worst aspects of this hereditary upper class. The medieval nobility ruled their world with (literally!) an iron fist. Anyone not a member of their class was totally unworthy of their consideration. The lower classes especially were there to be used and exploited, or brushed out of the way; they had no rights, no recourse (unless their overlord deigned to grant it), and were often not even really considered to be people at all. The warrior class did fight primarily among themselves—but this was of little advantage to the peasant who happened to be caught in the middle, since they also destroyed anything that got in their way.

There are parallels to this type of person in modern society. In terms of a class of people, Swords can represent powerful political figures such as dictators, extremist groups such as terrorist organizations (or the power interests who sponsor and use them), organized crime; in short, anyone or group who feels that their ends are all that matter—especially if they are in a position of power, or if they will use force or any other means available to get and keep power. On a personal level, Swords cards represent false friends, treacherous business associates, or others dangerous to the querent. In any case, the suit describes people who will always do what is best for themselves, rather than what is fair or just, and rarely if ever caring who gets hurt in the process.

People represented by Swords are those who are self-centered, and either carelessly or deliberately cruel. They are certainly not to be trusted, and may be violent as well. These are people who are out for their own interests, and have no concern for what happens to you as long as they get what they want. They will harm you for their own pleasure and help you only if doing so helps themselves more.

Events or situations represented by Swords are not merely obstacles in your path, but actively dangerous, and perhaps even deadly. In general terms Swords represents illness, natural disaster, or other serious and sometimes violent problems, including death. Even if the problem is not that serious, or obviated by other cards in the reading, Swords will at the least indicate frustration, anxiety, arguments, or tension.

If this suit represents the querent, then let the reader beware. The querent is not a nice person—certainly not in this situation, and perhaps in other ways as well. Note, however, that the rage and vindictiveness indicated by this suit may be caused by the situation. Other cards in the reading will tell you if the querent has a legitimate reason to be this angry (for example, if he or she has been badly wronged and is simply fighting back), or if this person is by nature a dangerous and untrustworthy individual.

In general, Swords is an ominous and unlucky suit, and when cards from this suit show up in a reading, something unpleasant is in the offing. What makes them even more dangerous is that Swords cards carry with them not only indications of trouble and misfortune, but also elements of power and authority. Swords people and situations have not only the willingness, but the means, to cause great harm.

Description of the Suit Symbol

Except for the Ace, Swords are most often depicted as double-bladed sabers, curved blades with a guard at the point or sheathed. Single swords, such as the Ace (or those in decks which are illuminated), are usually shown as unsheathed broadswords.

The swords are never shown as rapiers (a weapon of finesse!), but as battle swords, hacking and killing weapons, powerful military swords, and so forth. The symbolism is that there is enough power here that finesse is hardly necessary.

The Royal Court

The suit of Swords allegorizes absolute power corrupting absolutely.

KING OF SWORDS

꙳

The King of Swords represents a man of power and authority, or a situation that is potentially harmful.

꙳

Description

Most decks show a mature man *en garde* on a throne or chair. He is fully armored and wearing a helmet with a crown atop it. He holds a sword upright in his right hand; and his position seems to indicate that he's ready at any time to stand up and attack. His expression is grim and determined.

Meaning

The King of Swords is a man of authority and power, often in his own right, and certainly in terms of the querent's personal or professional life. He is someone accustomed to giving orders and seeing to it that they are obeyed. The querent will see him as someone whose motives are not always clear; he sometimes seems a powerful ally and at other times an unscrupulous enemy. Be warned, however, that whatever this man says or does, he is out to forward his own interests first, and will ride roughshod over anyone who gets in his way. This is a man who sits in judgement, both of situations and of those under his authority. Unlike the symbol of Justice in the Major Arcana, however, he holds no balanced scales. Justice in his view is whatever benefits himself.

If this card does not represent an actual person, then it does indicate that you are in an extremely precarious situation, perhaps even one of life and death. You are well advised to guard yourself diligently; there is a real and present danger.

In the Reading

Upright (or Positive): A man of power, authority and intelligence. A man in a position to issue and carry out judgements; perhaps someone with legal authority or political connections, etc. If the querent is male, the King of Swords may represent an ambitious man who can and will prove a dangerous rival, injuring either business or personal relationships. If the querent is a woman, she is warned not to get personally involved with this man: at the least, he will be worthless or incompatible; at the worst, potentially physically dangerous to her. The accompanying cards will define the nature of the danger.

If the card does not represent a person, then the situation itself is potentially harmful. Expect worry, grief, chagrin, even physical danger.

Reversed (or Negative): An evil man, or one of evil intent. Cruelty, perversity, barbarity. In effect, the same power and authority, but definitely used with intent to harm.

QUEEN OF SWORDS.

QUEEN OF SWORDS

The Queen of Swords represents a woman of power and authority, or a symbol of personal loss, emotionally devastating situations.

Description

A mature woman, crowned and regally robed. She may be either standing or seated on a throne. Like the King, she holds a sword upright in her right hand. Her left hand is usually raised in a gesture of judgement. Her expression is intent and may be seen as either stern and unyielding, or angry.

Meaning

Like the King, this is a woman of power and authority, with the intent of using it to forward her own purposes. She will be perceived by the querent as a woman who is malicious, domineering, or selfishly spiteful. If this card does not represent a person, it is a symbol of widowhood, personal loss, emotionally devastating situations.

(Note that the card of the King represents physical danger; the card of the Queen emotional danger.)

In the Reading

Upright (or Positive): A malicious, spiteful woman, and one who is in a position to do you great harm. She is both ruthless and cruel. If the querent is male, he is well advised not to establish any kind of personal relationship with this woman if he can help it. If the querent is female, the card is an indicator of betrayal by someone she thought was a friend.

If this card does not represent a person, then the indications are of bereavement and sadness, separation and privation, widowhood and mourning.

Reversed (or Negative): An evil woman, with the power to do harm and the evil intent as well. Malice, bigotry, deceit. A situation which will cause you intense unhappiness or, at the least, great embarrassment.

KNIGHT of SWORDS .

KNIGHT OF SWORDS

⊸֍⫷

The Knight of Swords represents someone who will undermine or hurt you, or a warning of enmity and opposition.

⫸֍⊸

Description

Most decks show a fully armored knight on a charging or rearing horse. He is challenging or charging an attacker or enemy; his expression is grim or even angry and indicates that he is determined to win in this confrontation. He carries his sword raised high in attack position.

Meaning

The Knight of Swords is a younger man with the same attributes as his symbolic parents; selfish, treacherous, self-serving and cruel. Because he is younger, it may not seem that he has the kind of power and authority needed to do harm. But within his own sphere of influence he does, and he is also likely to backed by others who can help him do even more harm (or escape the consequences of the harm he does). This is someone who is testing his ability to become what the King and Queen already are, so he is likely to be less subtle and more violent. A spy, an enemy, a bigot; someone who will undermine or hurt the querent. If this card does not represent a person, it does warn of enmity and opposition. If neighboring cards in the reading are negative, the Knight of Swords warns of destruction or death.

In the Reading

Upright (or Positive): A treacherous young man. A false friend. An individual who is clever and brave, and very active in his own interests. He is prepared to ride down anyone he sees as being in his way. He has distinct leadership qualities, and can convince others to follow him (willingly or otherwise), which makes him all the more dangerous to those he chooses to consider enemies. Note that one of the things that makes him dangerous is that even the querent may admire this person. It is best that you oppose rather than follow him if you can; his followers benefit no more than his enemies. If this card does not describe an actual person, it predicts conflict, opposition, and possibly destruction and death.

Reversed (or Negative): Wasteful extravagance. Imprudence, incapacity, poor leadership. A foolish or conceited person (or a warning against conceit or foolishness). Again, you are warned to watch your back; you have an influential and dangerous enemy, or are in a potentially explosive situation.

PAGE of SWORDS.

PAGE OF SWORDS

❧

The Page of Swords represents a person pretending to be a friend, bad news.

❧

Description

Most decks show a young man standing confidently, holding a sword upright in his right hand. Sometimes he holds the sword upright with both hands on the pommel. He usually is not shown wearing armor, but is well-dressed and often wears the same colors as the Knight. Many decks attempt to depict a sense of self-importance in this figure; the Page also tends to be somewhat effeminate. His attitude appears to be, in many decks, that of someone who is looking for an enemy, or expecting one to appear at any moment.

Meaning

A younger man or woman, less mature, but otherwise with the same qualities as the other court cards. The Page is not as powerful as the other court cards, but can be just as unpleasant: the qualities he or she displays are those of a prying, spiteful, malicious individual. Like his symbolic parents and the Knight, the Page can be attractive in his own way; eager, confident, active. But this young person is a master of innuendo, under-handedness, and the undercutting remark. The Page is a "hanger-on"; someone who attaches him or herself to power hoping it will rub off, or pretends to be connected to influence and power. He or she will pretend to be a friend, as long as it suits their interests; as a partner in any enterprise will hinder the querent either deliberately, or through carelessness and laziness.

If this is not a person, expect bad news, malicious rumor, betrayal, and treachery.

In the Reading

Upright (or Positive): A malicious, treacherous young man or woman. Someone who will hurt (or try to hurt) the querent out of envy or spite. If you are not their enemy, they are perfectly capable of making you one, whether or not you're aware of it (or do anything to warrant it). If the card does not represent a person, then beware of spying, malicious rumor, bad news coming or received. May also indicate sickness.

Reversed (or Negative): The same bad intentions, or bad news, intensified. Also, that they will happen when you are least prepared, and from a direction least expected.

The Pip Cards

The following ten cards are the number cards, or Pip Cards

ACE OF SWORDS

The Ace of Swords represents triumph by force.

Description

Most decks show a hand gripping an upright sword by the hilt. Near the top of the illustration, around the point of the sword, is a crown. Either the sword, or crown, or both are decorated with some form of living vines or branches, sometimes just with leaves, sometimes with fruit or berries as well.

Meaning

A card of triumph, in an almost excessive degree. It carries with it the concept of triumph by force: physical force, force of will, force of position or circumstances. You start this cycle as king of the mountain: you've won a tremendous victory or attained a high position, and you are (or will soon be) feeling both the euphoria and the power of your conquest. This is also a card of prosperity and fertility. The triumph can refer to any area of your life: profession, love, money, whatever endeavor you were engaged in. In effect, in this suit you (seem to!) start off where others finish: with what appears to be, and perhaps is for now, all your goals achieved.

In the Reading

Upright (or Positive): Triumph, prosperity, conquest, fertility. A birth (of a child, or an idea, or a new endeavor). Tremendous power used and/or now available, in any area you chose to use it, from love to hatred. Extreme feelings, both regarding this situation and others around you; excess in everything connected to it. You are riding high on the crest of the wave.

Reversed (or Negative): The same, but with disastrous results for the querent. You have still won a great victory, but you will very soon have reason to wish you hadn't, if you don't already. The beginning of tense relations and emotional conflicts with others and even yourself.

SWORDS (2) SWORDS

△ Peace Restored △

TWO OF SWORDS

The Two of Swords is generally favorable, indicating friendship and union.

Meaning

A generally favorable card, indicating friendship and union. An alliance with a comrade in arms to achieve a mutual goal; or, at the least, the recognition that there is a mutual goal to be attained. Care must still be taken, though, since Swords are not generally a good sign in human relationships and affairs; the friendship here is a qualified one. Consider this more an alliance based on mutual benefit to the querent and some other (person or group). At best, the alliance can be maintained only so long as the two of you don't get in each other's way; at the least, impartiality on the part of a possible opponent, or a possible stalemate which is being resolved by a joining of forces. If the card is negative, beware betrayal, either in this situation or in one to come.

In the Reading

Upright (or Positive): Friendship, union, alliance. Courage, harmony, even intimacy. Impartiality rather than open antagonism from a potential opponent, or a possible stalemate (for the opponent) which leaves you able to move. Or, opposition which will not last or is not significant enough to impede you.

Reversed (or Negative): Deceit, disloyalty, falsehood, disorder. Imposture and duplicity on the part of a seeming ally. Lies, treachery, dishonor.

THREE OF SWORDS

The Three of Swords indicates the disintegration of alliances.

Meaning

This is a card of severance, of separation. Alliances previously established will disintegrate due to quarrels, opposing interests, conflicts between the parties. It was not a stable alliance to begin with, being based on selfish interests for at least one if not both parties involved. Now it's coming apart. Protect your interests in this breakup, because that is what your former partner will definitely be doing. You have to stay on top of things; it will be a confusing and upsetting time, and things can go very wrong as a result of this breakup if you don't keep your head straight.

In the Reading

Upright (or Positive): Separation, severance, removal, divorce. Delays and ruptures in personal or business relationships. Dispersion of property and power. Quarrels.

Infidelity. Sorrow. A possible "love triangle": i.e., some other party (or some other event or interests) entering into the picture may be the reason for the breakup. The breakup will not be amicable; expect quarrels, anger, even hatred.

Reversed (or Negative): Confusion, mental disorder. Errors made, distractions. It may be very difficult to see clearly what to do; if so, your losses will be that much greater. This is the breakup of a partnership: keep your head clear or you could lose more than you should.

SWORDS (4) SWORDS

△ Rest From Strife △

FOUR OF SWORDS

The Four of Swords means contemplation and vigilance is needed, or a period of recuperation.

Meaning

You are going to have to work out your problems, and plan your future actions, alone from here. You need solitude and quiet; don't avoid it. This is a card of contemplation and vigilance; almost a hermit's retreat. It also indicates a necessary period of recuperation from the situation you just passed through. Take this time to work things out on your own and plan more wisely. Don't expect the highs you had up until now; as you've seen, they proved themselves no good for you. If you look for the same exaltation, you may find yourself in the same unpleasant situation.

In the Reading

Upright (or Positive): Solitude and quiet. Exile, retreat, need to plan and think. Careful planning will bring success against your enemy. Convalescence. Caution and precaution; economy and circumspection; all are necessary now.

Reversed (or Negative): Greed. Bad dreams. Perhaps a short illness or temporary financial problems. Envy and petty jealousy—either on your own part or that of others—may adversely affect your plans. Minor misfortunes as a result.

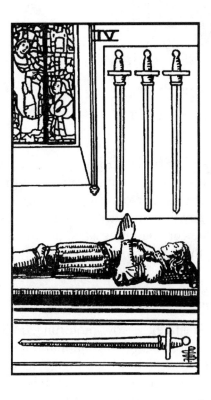

FIVE OF SWORDS

꧁꧂

The Five of Swords foretells the defeat of your plans, great loss, ruin, or misfortune.

꧁꧂

Meaning

This is a card of ruin and misfortune. It foretells the defeat of your plans, an unhappy or tragic situation, and/or great loss. Surrounding cards (ie: other events or people) may mitigate these losses; but you are heading into some very bad times, and about all you can do is try to get through them as best you can.

In the Reading

Upright (or Positive): Sorrow, mourning, tragic situation. Degradation, destruction, dishonor and loss in store for the querent. Possible hidden dangers, as well as those you can foresee. Discouragement and defeat.

Reversed (or Negative): The same. Your enemy had been overcome for a time, but is now the winner.

SWORDS (6) SWORDS

Earned Success

SIX OF SWORDS

The Six of Swords indicates a journey, or visitor or message.

Meaning

Here things begin to change, but whether for better or worse is uncertain at this time. You may take a journey, or receive a visitor or a message. Whatever happens, you are slowly moving out of the bad situation in which you recently found yourself. Note that some interpretations of this card also include "a proposal of love": either in a romantic sense, or in the sense of someone offering you their genuine allegiance. If the travel is actually from one physical place to another (as opposed to a change in your mental or emotional orientation), most interpretations agree that it will probably be by (or, considering modern possibilities, over) water.

In the Reading

Upright (or Positive): A journey whose destination is uncertain. A change of unknown effect. A message received. Escape; reprieve. The change may possibly render your enemy harmless. Sometimes this card brings luck despite earlier failures.

Reversed (or Negative): A confession, a declaration. Perhaps a proposal of love. In any case, a surprise.

SEVEN OF SWORDS

≈≈

The Seven of Swords means hope and renewed confidence.

≈≈

Meaning

This is a card of hope and renewed confidence. The worst seems to be over. If you base your confidence, and your plans, on your understanding of and experience with the situation, you may yet succeed. Be careful of overconfidence, and don't try to bluff. Your experiences have taught you what you need to know and your own strengths can carry you through. There's no need to push beyond that. Don't talk too much about what you need or plan to do; babbling will only aid your enemies.

In the Reading

Upright (or Positive): Hope and confidence. New attempts at overcoming previous failures which may very well succeed at this time. Possibly good advice (either your own or from some other source); instruction you can use to straighten things out.

Reversed (or Negative): Slander. A plan that may fail; annoyances. Overconfidence leading to instability in your affairs.

EIGHT OF SWORDS

The Eight of Swords warns of unexpected calamities.

Meaning

Another negative and dangerous card. In this case, you are warned of general and perhaps unexpected calamities, such as sickness or injury. You may also receive bad news, or take losses. You still have enemies out there, and they are still trying to defeat you. False friends may become your enemies. The one advantage of this card is that the problems are temporary in nature and may be avoided altogether if you take the proper precautions. This is a warning that things can go wrong; if you watch your back, you may keep it only a warning and not a fact. Check all your affairs carefully, and without delay.

In the Reading

Upright (or Positive): Sickness, injury. Bad news; a crisis in your affairs; conflict. Possible losses. The situation is temporary, however, and may perhaps be one you can prevent or avoid. Be on your guard.

Reversed (or Negative): Treachery and opposition, usually unexpected, or from an unexpected direction. Accident or fatality. Uncertainty.

NINE OF SWORDS

ᘓ𝍖ᘒ

The Nine of Swords foretells death, failure, utter despair.

ᘓ𝍖ᘒ

Meaning

The nine of swords is considered, in most interpretations, the worst card in the deck. It foretells death, failure, utter despair. Even among the best of cards, it can mean illness, loss of money or property, unhappiness. It means the presence of an unrelenting enemy, either an actual person or in the form of just plain bad luck. Projects influenced by this card are inevitably bound to bring you misfortune. The best you can hope for here is for the inner strength to weather the storm. Note: if you've done something you shouldn't (or are planning to) this card means you will be caught and punished: the unrelenting enemy may not necessarily be the evil one here if it is the querent who is the wrongdoer.

In the Reading

Upright (or Positive): Death, despair, utter failure. Delays and deceptions. An implacable enemy. Evil fate.

Reversed (or Negative): Shame, fear, doubt, suspicion. An unreliable person influencing your situation.

TEN OF SWORDS

❧

The Ten of Swords foretells of sorrow, tears and affliction either presently or soon to come.

❧

Meaning

The series of events which began in triumph ends in misery. The Ten of Swords foretells of sorrow, tears, and affliction either present or soon to come. It is not necessarily a card of death (as is the Nine), but it is one of pain, failure, and desolation. At the best, this card merely nullifies good luck; at the worst, it intensifies the misfortunes predicted by other unfavorable cards. Even friendships or other close relationships will be temporary, or insufficient to help you overcome this unhappy ending to your plans and schemes. Any gains will be brief ones. What is worse, this disastrous ending may undermine your confidence in yourself from now on. You will have to work hard to prevent that from happening to you.

In the Reading

Upright (or Positive): Tears, pain and sorrow in store for the querent. Affliction, misery and desolation. Ruin and misfortune. Insecure relationships with friends. Expect your plans to end in failure. All is lost.

Reversed (or Negative): A possible gain, but only a brief and temporary one. Any profit or success will also not be permanent.

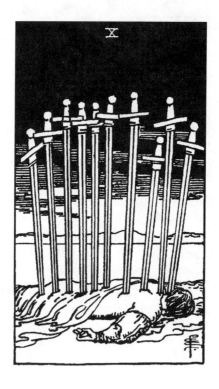

Cups

THE SUIT OF CUPS

The second strongest suit in the Minor Arcana, Cups is the exact opposite of its sister suit, Swords. Called the suit of love and happiness, Cups represents love in all its forms, not just the romantic. In a reading, these cards also signal the presence of genuine caring and concern for others, of kindness and healing (both emotional and physical), of friendship and strong attraction.

The symbol of the Cup originally represented the clergy in medieval society—the cup or chalice being that which held the sacramental wine. Since most religions use a cup or chalice in their rites, "clergy" can refer to any faith in modern reference. Just as Swords pictures the worst aspects of the warrior class, Cups describes the best aspects of the religious class. The allegory here is of selfless devotion, and even, in some situations, of divine protection.

In medieval times, positions of power within the church were reserved for the nobility, and the rulers of the church could be just as selfish and dangerous as the secular class from which they came. They are not the people represented by this suit, however. The reference is to the local, or parish priest, who usually came from the lower classes himself. The local priest had a personal understanding of the lives of the people he ministered to; he could, and often did, act as intercessor not only between his parishioners and God, but also between the powerless and the barons. He still had to submit to the authority of the higher-ups, both in the church and among the nobility—which is why this is the second strongest suit, not the first—but he did help those in his care when he could. The church also, for all its faults, functioned as a charitable institution, and often served as a sanctuary for members of all classes when they had no place else to turn.

In modern terms, Cups represents any individual or class of people who act out of love for others. As a class, Cups represents philanthropists, charitable organizations, humanitarian groups, and similar institutions, with the proviso that the reason for their activities is that they genuinely hope to benefit others, not because they have something to gain for themselves. On a personal level, Cups cards describe close family members, true friends, or lovers—anyone who sincerely cares about the querent. In general, the Cups suit reveals unselfish devotion toward an individual, or toward an ideal.

If a Cups card represents a person, it describes someone who is generous and affectionate by nature. This is someone upon whom you can depend in a crisis, certainly to offer emotional support and, if it is within their power to give it, other kinds of assistance as well. This does not mean that you're dealing with a pushover, however; it is possible for a nice person to get angry too, given cause. Their anger, however, will most often be in defense of someone or something they care about, and/or against some actual or threatened danger to what they love. Note also, however, that just because someone genuinely cares about you doesn't necessarily mean their advice will be good for you. Surrounding cards will reveal whether or not the love is wise as well as true.

Situations or events described by Cups are generally fortunate, and the suit represents good things in your life: love, happiness, good health, true friends, affectionate and pleasant surroundings or circumstances. In a reading, these cards indicate either happiness for the querent or, at the least, mitigation of unhappy circumstances.

When a Cups card represents the querent, then he or she is basically a nice person and probably an affectionate one as well (again, certainly in this situation and possibly in general). This suit also indicates that the querent is capable of strong positive feelings toward the people or situations with which he or she is currently involved. Again, surrounding cards will reveal if the querent is wise or misguided in his or her affections in this situation.

The curious aspect of this suit is how much it is affected by the querent's own attitude. While Cups refers to all aspects of your emotional life, most people getting readings do want to know about their chances for love and romance. Yet many of the interpretations of these cards indicate that people are wary about going for it. You'll find that Cups interpretations repeat over and again that the querent could be happy if only he or she would recognize and accept it.

In general, these cards are positive in all readings. At their best, they indicate strong alliances and people or circumstances surrounding the querent which will deliberately work in his or her favor. They may also mitigate the evils shown in ill-omened cards. At their worst, the love may be misguided, or the help offered not sufficient to overcome a really bad situation, but there is no ill-will shown by these cards, however, and they can often make some very bad situations much easier to endure.

Description of the Suit Symbol

In most decks, Cups are depicted as large and often elaborate chalices, richly decorated, and usually gold. These are standing chalices, with wide mouths, rising from a stem which can be easily encircled by the hand, and standing on a stable base. They give the impression of both richness and beauty; the symbolism suggests that it is with love that true wealth lies.

Note also that there is rarely any difficulty in determining upright from reverse in this suit, as the chalices are usually shown positioned in the same direction on all cards. Some suits also include depictions of water (this suit's corresponding element), either actually or symbolically, at least in the court cards and sometimes in the pip cards as well.

The Royal Court

The suit of Cups allegorizes true love, romantic or familial, and often selfless devotion.

KING of CUPS.

KING OF CUPS

The King of Cups represents a just and good man, or a situation involving justice, intelligence, or honor.

Description

Most decks show a mature man, seated on a throne. Sometimes the throne is shown at the shore, or actually floating on water. He may or may not be crowned; most decks show some kind of elaborate headgear with or without a crown. Usually this King is not shown wearing armor; if he is, it's generally only a token amount, such as just the breastplate. In most decks he is wearing royal robes.

He holds the cup or chalice in his right hand, held by the stem. In some decks he is holding it up as though displaying it to the viewer; in others it is resting on his knee. In many decks, he also holds a scepter in his left hand; whether or not he does, his left arm is resting on the arm of the throne. His attitude is relaxed and casual; he appears at ease with himself. The King's expression is generally mild; in all respects the aspect of this figure is at the least nonthreatening if not actually friendly.

Meaning

The King of Cups should bring to mind a paternal man, one who is just, and kindly disposed toward the querent. If he is not your father, he does fill the role of a fair and loving father, or has done so in the past. He is someone for whom you feel a genuine affection, and who displays that affection toward you. This is a man who can be trusted absolutely; he favors the querent, and tends to be kind and generous in his relationships in general. Most interpretations also describe the King of Cups as a cultivated and cultured man as well; interested in art and science, and possessing a creative intelligence. If this card does not represent an actual person, then circumstances themselves are highly favorable for whatever endeavor you have in mind.

In the Reading

Upright (or Positive): A just and honest man, who is or has been kindly disposed toward the querent. Responsible and mature, he displays paternal feelings toward the querent. He is intelligent and probably cultured and well-educated as well; and as a result has skills and connections which you need at this time. His appearance in the reading indicates that he is willing to help you in some way; or will be willing if asked for help. If the card does not represent a person, then the situation involves justice, honor, learning and understanding, intelligence and intelligent action; in short, authority fairly used.

Reversed (or Negative): A deceitful man; one who cannot be trusted. A dishonest, double-dealing man who will trick you, or cause losses in personal relationships or career. Injustice, vice, scandal in the offing.

Note that negative readings on the court cards are still positive in their own way. They indicate that this is someone that you do or will love or trust, but you are being warned not to, for your own good.

QUEEN OF CUPS.

QUEEN OF CUPS

〜∿〜

The Queen of Cups represents a mother figure, intelligent and cultured, or an environment in which you do, or should, feel secure.

〜∿〜

Description

Most decks show a mature woman, sometimes standing, most often seated on a throne. She is richly dressed, often robed, and almost always wearing a crown. The Queen holds the cup in her right hand; if she is standing, she is holding it out toward the viewer as though offering it. If seated, the cup may be resting on one knee, or held in both hands. Some decks show the Queen's cup with a rounded cover. If the Queen is holding the cup in only one hand, then her other hand holds a scepter, or some other sign of rank. In almost all decks, she is looking at the cup, as if contemplating it, or seeing visions in it. As with the King, her expression is mild; she is often depicted as smiling, perhaps friendly, even affectionate.

Meaning

The Queen of Cups should evoke the image of a kind and generous woman who has a maternal interest in the querent. If she is not your own mother, she is someone who is prepared to assist, advise, and mother you. She is a woman for whom you feel affection and even love, and with whom you feel accepted, protected, and emotionally secure. The Queen of Cups is a loving wife, good mother, and devoted friend. As a person, she is intelligent and cultured; she is someone who knows how to love wisely, and who can (and will if asked) wisely advise the querent in affairs of the heart. Her characteristics are a loving intelligence, wisdom, and personal virtue. She may also be something of a visionary; but her visions are tempered by mature judgement and tend to be accurate.

If the querent is a man, this card represents a true and trustful wife, or his current or potential true love. If the querent is a woman, the Queen may be either a confidant or a rival in love (the surrounding cards will tell which); but even if she is a rival, she is a kind one, and will play fair.

If this card does not represent a person, then the situation is one in which the querent feels, or should feel, emotionally secure, safe, and even protected. This card describes a situation in which there are no hidden traps or unsuspected enmities; you are among people you can trust, and in a situation in which you can feel at home.

In the Reading

Upright (or Positive): A maternal female, who evokes feelings of affection or love. An honest, devoted female friend or relative who will perform a service for the querent. A good mother; a perfect spouse. If not a person, then a situation in which you feel emotionally secure. Success, happiness, pleasure. Wise choices, especially in personal relationships.

Reversed (or Negative): An untrustworthy or perverse woman. Vice, dishonor, depravity, meddling.

KNIGHT OF CUPS

KNIGHT of CUPS.

~~~

The Knight of Cups most often represents a lover, or the messenger of true love.

~~~

Description

Most decks show a young man riding a horse. The horse is in parade dress and position. The young man may or may not be wearing armor; either way, he is well-dressed. Sometimes he also has a hunting horn hanging by a shoulder strap; if not, he may have a winged cap. Either way, the symbolism is of a messenger of some kind. He carries the cup in his right hand, holding it out to one side, or out in front of him over the horse's head, and looking at or even into it. The Knight is generally shown in a country setting.

Meaning

A young man with the same qualities as his symbolic parents. If the card represents a person, this is someone with a fraternal interest in the querent. He is honest, intelligent, willing to help you in any way he can; a true and dependable friend, or even a lover. If the reading indicates he is a lover, he is someone you can safely allow yourself to love; even if the relationship should break up at some future point, this is someone who would make every attempt not to hurt you. If he is not a lover, then he is someone who can advise you on the true nature of the person you are interested in. Like the Queen, he may also be something of a dreamer; in this case he is not a visionary, but someone with imagination, and that allows him to understand other people's feelings as well as his own.

If this is not a person, then expect a message or an invitation; either will be positive and the situation one you can trust. The Knight of Cups is also interpreted for either sex as being the messenger of true love.

In the Reading

Upright (or Positive): Honest and intelligent young man who is friendly toward the querent. A brother, friend, or lover. Good advice, a message, a visit, or an invitation. True love; reciprocated love.

Reversed (or Negative): A treacherous, deceitful young man. Trickery, swindling, fraud, lies. Trust betrayed. Heartbreak; emotional harm to the querent.

PAGE of CUPS.

PAGE OF CUPS

⚬⚬

The Page of Cups is a person who will render an important service for you, or represents a message or an arrival.

⚬⚬

Description

A young man, well-dressed, stands in a relaxed position, holding the cup in one hand. Some decks show him holding the cup out as though presenting it to someone. Other decks show him obviously in possession of the cup, holding it up to admire it. He is often shown smiling, and almost always shown looking at the cup.

Meaning

A young man or woman, possibly your son or daughter (or someone who responds to you in that way) or brother or sister (usually a younger sibling). A sensitive young person with generally the same qualities as his or her elders, but with not as much "pull." The appearance of this card in the reading indicates that there is someone with whom you are at this time connected, and who will render an important service for you. If not a person, read this as a message, an arrival, possibly a birth.

In the Reading

Upright (or Positive): A sensitive young man or woman, one who is closely connected to you, such as a son or daughter, a brother, sister or cousin, a long-time friend, old schoolmate, or childhood sweetheart. He or she will perform a needed service for you. A studious, intelligent young person. News, a message, arrival of someone or something. A birth, either of a child or of an idea or enterprise. A promising start.

Reversed (or Negative): Deceit, seduction, false flattery, deception.

The Pip Cards

The following ten cards are the number cards, or Pip Cards

ACE OF CUPS

*The Ace of Cups
symbolizes fertility,
celebrations,
consummation of a
worthy union.*

Description

Most decks show a single large cup. Like the Queen's cup, it usually has a rounded and often decorated cover. Some decks simply show the cup; others show a hand holding the cup, either grasping it by the stem or simply displaying it resting on the palm. If there is a hand shown holding the cup, it is usually issuing from a cloud. If there is any other symbolism in the background of the illustration, it will have to do with water, such as a sea beneath the cup and/or fountains arching water from the cup.

Meaning

The Ace of Cups symbolizes fertility, celebrations, and merrymaking, and consummation of a worthy union. The beginning here is of a marriage or other partnership which will be happy in its inception and of benefit to both parties. The appearance of the Ace in the reading also foretells the possibility of such a union; it predicts the beginning of a true and lasting love.

In the Reading

Upright (or Positive): Fertility. Abundance in all things, especially in love. The beginning of love; or consummation of a union both appropriate and beneficial to all concerned. True love, joy, contentment. Merriment and celebration.

Reversed (or Negative): Instability. A false heart; disappointments in relationships. A change in relationships, most likely due to these things. Can mean infidelity and deceit.

TWO OF CUPS

The Two of Cups symbolizes a partnership, a marriage, a union, all based in harmony.

Meaning

One added to One: the Two of Cups symbolizes a partnership, a marriage, a union. Whatever the relationship described, whether a new one upcoming or an old one strengthened, it will be based on harmony.

In the Reading

Upright (or Positive): Love, friendship, affinity, affection. Union, partnership. Mutual sympathy, concord, harmony. Most often refers to a union of the sexes; can in some readings refer to other unions or partnerships which you are considering joining or in which you are already involved.

Reversed (or Negative): The same positive things. Negative cards surrounding it can delay this influence, or put obstacles in the path of the people involved. But in the end, even negative influences cannot change it. This is a union that is meant to be, and good for both you and any other(s) involved.

III de Agua

III of Water

III de Água

Ψ

THREE OF CUPS

The Three of Cups is a card of success and victory in business or relationships.

Meaning

This is a card of success and fulfillment. Some affair or enterprise in which you have been involved has been or will soon be concluded in plenty and merriment, to the complete satisfaction of all concerned. If a romantic relationship began earlier on, it is at this point that you are told both have fallen in love.

In the Reading

Upright (or Positive): Success, perfection, plenty, merriment. Happy issue, fulfillment. Victory; achievement of great things.

Reversed (or Negative): Also success and achievement, but in purely physical terms. Excess; gratification of sensual pleasures. Achievement in small things.

THREE OF CUPS

THE DRESSING OF THE SACRED SPRING

CUPS 4 CUPS

Blended Pleasure

FOUR OF CUPS

The Four of Cups represents a friendly warning; your own negative outlook is keeping you from attaining or appreciating everything you need or could hope for.

Meaning

This card represents a friendly warning. You are told that everything you need, every good thing you could possibly hope for, is available to you, but your own dissatisfaction or negative outlook is keeping you from recognizing, appreciating, or taking advantage of it. You are so intent on your displeasure that you are missing fulfillment. One interpretation calls this the "bachelor/old maid" card, and states that the reason for the long-delayed marriage is because of the querent's "fussy disposition." In effect, the warning is the same. The reason you are discontent is because you choose to be, not because your life is truly unfulfilling.

In the Reading

Upright (or Positive): Displeasure, dissatisfaction. Weariness with life. Imaginary vexations, disgust. All leading to your own unwillingness to accept good things being offered. Discontent and unwarranted suspicions.

Reversed (or Negative): New relationships, new acquaintances, new instruction, novelty. An unforeseen event.

CUPS 5 CUPS

Loss in Pleasure

FIVE OF CUPS

The Five of Cups tells you you are seeing only the losses and not the gains; it's up to you to see the positive.

Meaning

Here again, it is your attitude which affects your outlook on the situation. Five is a card of losses *and* gains, but the probability is that you are seeing only the losses and not the gains. You have the opportunity for happiness, if you will see the positive side of what you have. Five also predicts a union, possibly a marriage, and warns that whether or not it's happy will be up to you. Following from the Four, the Five suggests that the reason you're unhappy is because you deliberately (even if unconsciously) took the down side to prove that your discontent or disillusionment was correct. You took the lesser of two choices, or threw away positive gains; in effect, you cut off your nose to spite your face. You could have been happy and fulfilled. You still can be. It's entirely up to you. This is also a card of indecision; an inability to make up your mind on important issues. Sometimes the Five portends a change in surroundings, due to your desire to escape these issues; in effect, instead of dealing with the situation, you run away.

In the Reading

Upright (or Positive): An upcoming union; a possible marriage or partnership. There have been losses, but also gains. The losses are only partial, and the sadness only momentary. Also, inheritance, but not as much as the querent wanted or expected. A change of plans, a change in surroundings or personal situation.

Reversed (or Negative): Bitterness, frustration, an unhappy marriage; all due to poor choices or unrealistic expectations. Surprises, false promises, false projects.

SIX OF CUPS

The Six of Cups is a card of memories and looking back at when you were happy; it shows that you can relearn happiness.

Meaning

Your earlier discontent with current situations leads naturally to this card. Six describes thoughts of past loves and past happinesses. It is a card of memories and looking back, of remembering times when you were happy, in the way a child is happy. Again, how these memories will affect you depends on you. Don't brood over what you've "lost"; if you use these memories to relearn how to be happy, to regain your innocence, and—most important—to remind you that you have been happy, you can be happy again. In a particularly fortunate reading, the appearance of this card can indicate that someone or some event will force you to recognize the good in your life.

In the Reading

Upright (or Positive): Memories, looking back (especially on childhood); thoughts of past loves. Happiness coming from the past, from thoughts of things that have vanished. A promise for the future; of renewal, happiness and love to come.

Reversed (or Negative): New friends, new knowledge, new environment. Changes in attitudes and relationships. Things to come soon; something important soon to happen.

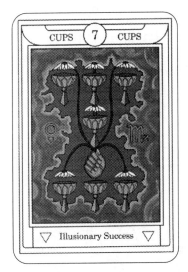

SEVEN OF CUPS

The Seven of Cups represents imagination and visions, either fantastic or reflective.

Meaning

This is a card of imagination and visions. Some of the visions may be on the side of the fantastic: fairy dreams, castles in the air. Others may be reflective; others close to, but never quite attaining the status of actual plans. Basically you're simply daydreaming, not about anything definite, but simply letting your imagination take its own course. Most interpretations suggest that this is a necessary process, especially at this time: clearing your mind of old ideas or misconceptions and examining different possibilities and potentials, however remote. It can lead to the creation of new and happier goals.

In the Reading

Upright (or Positive): Abundance of fresh but indefinite ideas or images in the mind of the querent, but nothing permanent or substantial. Daydreaming; castles in the air. Unfocused meditation. Contemplation; imagination.

Reversed (or Negative): Determination, resolution, strong desires and plans, planning and projects.

EIGHT OF CUPS

☙❧

The Eight of Cups tells you you will get what you've hoped for, but you may be being overcautious.

❦

Meaning

The meanings here are contradictory. The Eight of Cups refers to a situation, event, or enterprise in which you have been involved or which you are planning. It suggests that things will turn out well; in fact, you're being told you will receive what you've hoped for. But it also indicates that you're displaying too much caution, and that doing so will lose for you what you hope to gain. In this case, it's not that you can't see the good things you have, but because you're too shy, too unsure of yourself or your personal worth, or too timid to make your move. And if you don't make your move, you may lose what you've worked and hoped for for so long.

There is also an interpretation, which has worked in practical readings, which adds that the matter at hand is not as important as it appears, for good or bad, and that taking action on it will reveal its actual value and make it decline in importance so that you can get on with other things. Again, make your move and you'll find that the situation is not as intimidating as it seems from a distance. Either way, success is waiting; whether or not you get what you want is up to you.

In the Reading

Upright (or Positive): Fulfillment of a wish, but also mildness, timidity, modesty. The querent is advised that honor might be best served by seizing the day, rather than backing away from it. A matter which looms as a large problem in the querent's mind is revealed as having much lesser consequence, for good or bad, once finally acted upon. Disappointment if the querent does not act on the matter.

Reversed (or Negative): Great happiness and joy. Feasting, pleasure. Most often refers to an event the querent knows about and has either anticipated or planned; surrounding cards will reveal whether other events or people will make this event as pleasurable as hoped, or will detract from it.

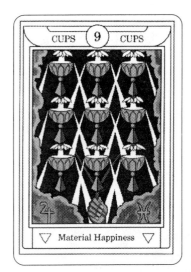

NINE OF CUPS

꧁ ꧂

*The Nine of Cups
says everything you
hoped for will soon
come to be, triumph,
complete success.*

꧁ ꧂

Meaning

There is no negative reading in this card at all. It is a
card of triumph, of complete success, almost of satiety.
Everything you hoped and planned for has or will very
soon come to be, and it is or will be as good if not better
than you dreamed it would. This is sometimes called
"the wish card": it promises fulfillment, harmony and
success in the projects described by other cards in the
reading. If there are unfavorable cards in the reading,
they may retard this ultimate success, but the obstacles
will be a only temporary annoyance. You have done
everything right up to now, and people and/or events
are also conspiring in your favor. This is your hour.

In the Reading

Upright (or Positive): Triumph, victory. Contentment
and even satiation for the querent. Success, advantage,

complete satisfaction in events and/or in the completion and outcome of your plans. Usually refers to material success and freedom from want, but can refer to other types of situations as well. General well-being as the result. Difficulties surmounted and overcome.

Reversed (or Negative): Interpretations vary for this reading. Some indicate truth, liberty, and loyalty. Others indicate disappointments due to imperfections and mistakes; some interpretations include both. In effect, all things are going well but you can still muck it up if you really try hard enough.

X de Agua

X of Water

X de Água

♓ ♆ ☽

TEN OF CUPS

The Ten of Cups describes real love: contentment, domestic bliss, satisfaction in your accomplishments.

Meaning

This card describes what real love is all about and what it should lead to: contentment, domestic bliss, satisfaction in your accomplishments and relationships. You are surrounded by those you love and those who love you, and the things that matter to you matter also to them, and vice versa. The Ten of Cups creates a picture of peace and harmony created by people sharing their lives and caring for each other. Picture cards in the reading may identify the other people who are involved in this state of bliss, or reveal a person who is watching out for your interests. The Ten is not only a favorable card but an influential one: it strengthens good cards in the reading and negates negative ones.

In the Reading

Upright (or Positive): The perfection of human love and friendship; true companionship and fulfillment in relationships. Love of home and satisfaction in your own accomplishments. Also success, but in this case not necessarily material; a happy family life, honors, esteem.

Reversed (or Negative): Sorrow, strife, disputes. Indignation and violence, possibly emotional. A false heart.

Coins

THE SUIT OF COINS

The third suit of the Minor Arcana, Coins symbolizes material wealth, enterprise, business and commerce, and worldly prestige.

Coins originally represented the merchant class in medieval society. The merchants engaged in manufacturing, dealing in commodities, and trade, both local and foreign. In these activities, they were also an influence for change, and their way of doing business not only impacted on their own society, but still affects the way people think and act in our own times. It was the merchants, for example, who established and promoted the concept of international trade. It was the merchants who evolved our money-based economy. Prior to their influence, people traded in kind for goods or services, but merchants dealt in coin and cash; it was a more convenient and efficient way of doing business. They were also responsible for the establishment of banks and bookkeeping systems, as well as commercial law.

Merchants were originally a kind of middle class in the medieval social order; they were not bound to the land, as were serfs, but they were not of royal blood nor under the protection of the church. Over time, however, the merchants created their own social status. They banded together into guilds, which were initially organized for self-protection and mutual benefit, but which eventually gave them tremendous power and influence. Because of the guilds, the merchants had a monopoly on trade, and that, plus their wealth, gave them a considerable voice in government affairs.

In our modern definition, then, Coins would represent big business, big banking, national and international commerce. These are the powerful commercial interests whose influence on world affairs can sometimes outweigh that of authorized governments. On a personal level, Coins depicts very wealthy and influential people; in general, those who not only have money, but who understand its power and influence and are prepared to use it.

If a card from this suit represents a person, he or she will be an entrepreneur; highly successful in business or finance; and/or someone canny in the ways of money and commerce. Coins ususally represents someone who is personally wealthy, but in any case will signal the presence of an individual who controls large amounts of money (as a banker, a broker, a financier). In a reading, this may be someone who can or will provide money for the querent. A Coins person is also likely to be someone the querent admires and respects, primarily because of his or her social status and wealth.

Circumstances represented by Coins are those involving material wealth, money, or money matters.

Coins is a suit of wealth, of social status (especially that derived from wealth or property), possession of material things, and prosperity in general. The suit also carries with it the suggestion or possibility of inherited wealth or status. The fact that these cards appear in a reading means that these advantages and influences exist to some extent in the querent's environment. At best, it indicates a very good possibility that some of that real wealth is going to wind up in the querent's possession; at the least, Coins in a reading predicts relief from debt, or from other problems caused by lack of money. In some readings these cards can also indicate that your current problems can be solved by an infusion of hard cash; whether that's good or bad depends on whether or not you can in fact get your hands on some money.

If this suit represents the querent, then he or she is either very rich or destined to be; or, as above, is someone who controls large sums of money in some way (which doesn't necessarily mean he or she is wealthy. Bank tellers handle large sums of money too). If the querent is not in such a position at this time, they are at least money-smart. This is someone who understands how to use money, how to make money, and how to employ its power.

Coins is a very worldly suit, little concerned with matters of the heart or spirit. It represents commercial or financial wisdom and usually temporal influence as well. It also indicates that business and finance, or at least, the things of this world, are a priority for the people or in the circumstances described by the reading.

Description of the Suit Symbol

Most decks show a golden disc, with a petal-style design repeated in concentric circles within. Some show actual pentacles: an upright pentagram in the center of a circle or disc. A number of decks which do not show a pentacle do have a five-sided design somewhere within the Coin, either in the center circle or in the design as a whole, hence the name Pentacles. The symbolism here is not only that of actual cash, in the form of gold coins, but of a degree of magickal power and protection as well. Remember also the interpretation of the number Five: adventure, excitement, the influence of worldly matters, and change.

The Royal Court

The suit of Coins allegorizes real wealth, worldly affairs, and often political or other forms of worldly influence and power.

KING of PENTACLES.

KING OF COINS

The King of Coins represents power and influence, a man interested in sponsoring the arts and sciences, albeit profit oriented.

Description

The King of Coins may or may not be crowned; if not, he is generally represented as a well-dressed, prosperous merchant. He may also be wearing some kind of jewelry (such as a gold-chain necklace) almost as a badge of office. He is seated on a throne or handsome chair; in many decks, his chair is decorated with some kind of real or mythical animal figure, such as a lion, a griffin, a bull, or an eagle (again, symbols of royalty, and temporal or magical power).

His attitude is at the same time proud, yet casual. This is someone comfortable with his position of power and who takes it as his due. He usually holds the coin upright in his right hand, as if showing it off to the viewer; in some decks, he also holds a scepter in his left hand. Many decks, even those which show this figure crowned and even armored, also show some kind of pouch at his side, representing a money bag.

Meaning

The King of Coins should call to mind a mature man, both wealthy and courageous. Like the King of Swords, he represents power, but in a more positive sense. He is firmly established in his own right, and can—and does—control the reins of government. He is also personally gifted, and/or interested in those who are. He will use his influence to sponsor the arts and sciences, with, no doubt, profit as his goal in many cases, but also for their own sake. This is someone who is personally well-enough established that he can be a patron of the arts; in that, he also represents the kind of society which is stable enough that art and science can flourish. If this card represents a person, he is the personification of the "enlightened monarch," both wise and powerful. He will be a man whom the querent admires for both his successes and his personal refinement. If the card represents a situation, then it predicts financial security and the kind of stable situation in which culture can flourish.

In the Reading

Upright (or Positive): A wealthy, powerful, and cultured man, who can provide wise counsel, help, and inspiration. A man of refinement, knowledgeable about money and finance, and a true patron of the arts and sciences. He may be either well-disposed toward the querent, or indifferent; but he is in either case highly unlikely to be antagonistic. The other cards in the reading will reveal his current attitude, and may also reveal what you must do to acquire this man's patronage if you need it. If this is not an actual person, the card is a symbol of enterprise and worldly glory, representing intelligence and business acumen. It may also represent personal gifts or talents, especially mathematical, and success in the areas of finance or social status. One interpretation also adds success through gambling, or through inheritance.

Reversed (or Negative): A dangerous man, and one the querent will do well to avoid. In business, he can be an absolutely ruthless competitor. If not a person, the card signifies doubt, weakness, fear, despair. Danger to the querent. Vice and perversity; corruption and evil intentions; conceit.

QUEEN oᶠPENTACLES

QUEEN OF COINS

❧

The Queen of Coins represents a regal and respected woman, or security, wisdom, prudence and wealth.

❧

Description

Usually depicted as a mature woman, well-dressed; she may or may not be crowned. Many decks show the Queen standing, supporting her weight on one leg or leaning against a decorative chair or throne. As with the King, she holds the coin aloft in her right hand, displaying it to the viewer; she is generally shown looking at the coin and totally occupied with it. If seated, she holds the coin in both hands, and is also contemplating it, as if seeing images within it. She sometimes holds a scepter in her left hand.

The Queen is often shown smiling; she is confident in her role and presents a kindly or pleasant attitude, but note that in most decks, the queen is paying absolute attention to the money.

Meaning

A regal and respected woman, known for her generous nature but never someone you can fool or take advantage of. She has respect for money, but is not ruled by it; a wise and prudent manager who provides an example to others of how best to use and distribute real wealth and be comfortable with it. Like the King, she is intelligent, and she has a greatness of soul which commands respect and admiration among both her peers and those she rules. If this card does not represent an actual person, then it describes a situation of well-ordered comfort, which comes not merely from having financial security, but in knowing how to use money wisely. The card also represents hope in the form of the ability—and knowledge that you have the ability—to overcome obstacles with prudence and wisdom.

In the Reading

Upright (or Positive): A kind and generous woman, an excellent and careful manager, with both intelligence and intuitive knowledge. Like the King, she may either favor the querent, or she may be indifferent. She is attractive and very persuasive; she knows how to get her own way, not through "feminine wiles" but simply because she knows what she's doing. If not a person, the card represents security, wisdom and prudence, wealth, and even opulence.

Reversed (or Negative): A suspicious woman, distrusting all around her, and mistrusted in return. An interfering woman, one who needs to control situations at any cost. If not a person, the card represents a situation of suspicion, fear, even evil. A suspenseful situation, one in which the querent cannot be certain who to trust, or if anyone can be trusted.

**KNIGHT OF
COINS**

∾⋙⋘∾

*The Knight
of Coins represents
a young man of
great potential, or
unfulfilled
expectations,
quarrels.*

⋙⋙⋘⋘

Description

Most decks show a young man on horseback; he is usually, but not always, wearing armor. In decks where the King and Queen are dressed as merchants rather than royalty, so is the Knight. In many decks he is not holding the coin; it is suspended in the air either in front of or behind him. Either way, he is looking directly at it, even if he has to turn in his saddle to see it. If the coin is in his hand, he is holding it up as if to exhibit it, but is not seriously contemplating it. The horse may be shown walking, or at parade rest; in any case, it is not charging. This is not a young man doing battle for his family or ideals; the imagery here is of travel or departure.

Meaning

The Knight of Coins exhibits the same qualities as his parents, but also includes elements of moving, either arrival, or departure, or travel. This is a less mature image than the King and Queen; he has their potential, but lacks their experience. He may still be a nice person, but not as dependable, and sometimes a disappointment to himself and others close to him. He may be impatient at times, and less willing to assume his responsibilities. Whether this is a permanent trait, or one he will eventually outgrow, depends on other cards in the readings. If this card does not represent a person, then you are being told that you could be more than you are if you'd simply settle down and work at it.

In the Reading

Upright (or Positive): A young man with an adventurous spirit. Possesses great potential, but does not fulfill it, at least not yet. A materially minded person, one less likely to look beyond the surface; an adventurer, a gambler. Given a task to perform, he has courage and can be responsible, but is not yet able to set his own goals and follow them. If not a person: a departure or arrival; possible discord or quarrels, usually concerning unfulfilled expectations.

Reversed (or Negative): An idle young man, or one who is negligent or irresponsible. Carelessness, discouragement, stagnation, apathy. If not a person, may indicate being unemployed or discouraged. This card may also show a lack of focus on the part of the querent; the inability to choose goals or work toward them wisely.

PAGE OF COINS

~~~

The Page of Coins is a scholary young man or woman, artistic and refined, or it can mean good news and enjoyments.

~~~

Description

Most decks show a young man standing in a field or other country setting. He is well-dressed and to all appearances very pleased with himself. His position varies. In some cases he holds the coin up in one hand as if showing it off, and he is admiring it. His left hand is either gesturing at the ground or hooked in his belt; the stance is almost that of the Magician. In other decks, he holds the coin up in both hands, or balancing it on the tips of his fingers. In either case, he is obviously pleased with himself and engaged in admiring his possession of the coin.

Meaning

A young man or woman, or perhaps a child, again with the potential for the same qualities as his or her symbolic parents. This is a young person of obvious refinement; like his parents appreciative of the arts, but more sensitive, both in the sense of awareness of others' needs and in his or her own vulnerability to hurt. The rapt interest in the coin is generally intended to symbolize the scholar; someone so intent on what he is learning—and on his ability to learn it—that he is less aware of reality and somewhat impractical. If this card does not represent a person it indicates that you are about to receive some kind of news or message. If the card represents the querent, it indicates ambition and a need to succeed, especially on a worldly level.

In the Reading

Upright (or Positive): Scholarly, reflective young man or woman; a dreamer. Intelligent, versed in and appreciative of the arts, refined, and sensitive. Good news, and/or the bearer of good tidings; enjoyment, worldly pleasure or satisfaction, luxury.

Reversed (or Negative): A banal or coarse person; selfish and self-involved. A prodigal; liberality, dissipation. A bearer of bad news; disappointment, pain or distress for the querent; waste of material or potential.

The Pip Cards

The following ten cards are the number cards, or Pip Cards

ACE ⚬ PENTACLES

ACE OF COINS

❧

The Ace of Coins is the card of attainment, new enterprises are destined for success.

❧

Description

Most decks simply show a single large coin in the center of the card, usually with some kind of decorative design growing out of the top and bottom. In some decks, the illustration repeats the theme of a divine revelation: a huge hand coming out of a cloud, holding the coin balanced in the palm.

Meaning

The Ace is the card of attainment. The new enterprise which you are now beginning, or will soon begin, is destined for success; the success will most probably be measured in material gain of one kind or another (such as money, status, fame, or some combination of these).

The card predicts success for your new venture no matter what the surrounding cards suggest, but with this proviso: if surrounding cards are negative, your success will bring with it unhappiness and jealousy; the evil aspects of wealth and attainment. Either way, however, it predicts prosperity and material gain.

In the Reading

Upright (or Positive): The beginning of a new enterprise whose success is assured. Contentment, attainment, wealth, great happiness, triumph.

Reversed (or Negative): The same attainment and prosperity, but with pain, or at the least without peace of mind.

TWO OF COINS

❧

The Two of Coins signifies good fortune, gaiety and fun, or perhaps good news, a warning to juggle financial affairs.

❧

Meaning

The Two signifies good fortune; also gaiety, and fun. It also suggests that the querent can expect news of some kind; most probably a message in writing. In a negative reading it warns of a necessity to juggle financial affairs, play off one advantage or situation against another (such as robbing Peter to pay Paul), with a degree of uncertainty as to how things will ultimately work out. Even in a favorable reading, however, this card suggests some difficulties in store for the querent.

In the Reading

Upright (or Positive): Good fortune. Gaiety and fun. News, messages (most likely written) received or forthcoming. Obstacles and difficulties; of what nature and how serious will be shown by other cards in the reading. Possible embarrassment. Problems in establishing financial security or wealth.

Reversed (or Negative): A distasteful experience. Forced gaiety, pretense of enjoyment. Exchange of letters. Juggling of finances and affairs. Doubt, worry, uncertainty.

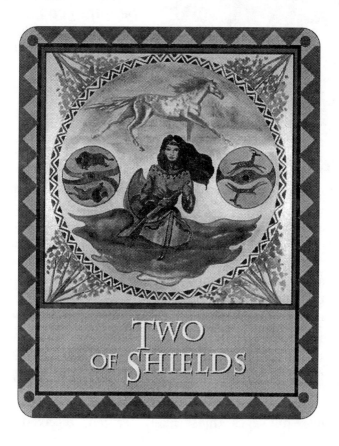

III de Tierra

III of Earth

III de Terra

THREE OF COINS

The Three of Coins describes proficiency in a craft, profession or trade, and that the skill could prove profitable.

Meaning

Again, this is a card of success, but with a different application. The Three of Coins describes proficiency in a craft, profession, or trade, and predicts the rewards which can be earned from that proficiency. If this card describes the querent, then he or she has prepared (or is preparing, depending on the position in the reading) themselves to earn a good living, and the presence of this card in the reading indicates that the choice of profession will result in success. If the card describes a situation or future event, you're being told that acquiring a saleable skill will result in ultimate success. It also suggests that the querent has the potential to learn such a skill, which is no small piece of good news in many cases!

In the Reading

Upright (or Positive): Enterprise, commerce. Skilled labor or the acquiring of skills; ability, craftsmanship. Success in trade or business. Personal nobility; rise in prestige; renown and glory.

Reversed (or Negative): Mediocrity, in both work and other areas; pettiness; weakness.

FOUR OF COINS

The Four of Coins is a card of possessions, feeling there is a need to protect these possessions.

Meaning

Four is a card of possessions and of holding on to what you have. The possessions are yours by right; you earned or inherited them. (And note here that "inherited" possessions also include skills or talents). The card also suggests the feeling, on the part of the querent, that there is a need to guard or protect these possessions. Other cards in the reading will indicate whether or not that feeling is justified. The card also cautions that while resting on your laurels may be comfortable, it is not a way to go forward or prepare for the future.

In the Reading

Upright (or Positive): Possessions, gifts. Holding on to what you have. Legacy or inheritance. Satisfaction in personal status; taking pleasure in your current situation. Also; a settled situation, in business or in personal affairs; few worries. Good feelings about the future.

Reversed (or Negative): Opposition, suspense, delays, obstacles. Possible loss. Possible quarrels, particularly with people close to the querent (such as quarrels over possessions or inheritances).

FIVE OF COINS

༄ ༄

The Five of Coins warns there could be disaster in business, material trouble, losses, or poverty.

༄ ༄

Meaning

This card is a warning; there is a slight potential for success in business, but there is a much greater potential for disaster. Even in a positive reading, the Five suggests material trouble, losses, or poverty. The querent is or soon will be in a situation where money is tight, and/or where material gains or possessions that he or she counted on will fall through. In some cases the problems may be caused by circumstances beyond your control; in others, they may be your own doing. Either way, you will have to watch your step to avoid ruin.

In the Reading

Upright (or Positive): Possible brief gain in business, but leading to losses unless great care is taken. Financial troubles; destitution. Want and poverty, loneliness, sudden loss.

Reversed (or Negative): Disorder, discord, chaos, ruin. Profligacy, imprudence, disgrace.

SIX OF COINS

The Six of Coins says the previous problems are solved; it describes you as being a person who cares about others and will use your prosperity to help.

Meaning

In this card the querent's previous problems are resolved. The indications are that the querent is about to begin a projector enterprise which is worthy of praise (as, for example, performing a charitable act); but the card also suggests that he or she will have the ability and wherewithal to do this praiseworthy thing. The six describes or predicts abundance of material worth and enough to spare. It also describes the querent as being someone who cares enough about others to use his or her prosperity as a means of helping others as much as possible.

In the Reading

Upright (or Positive): A good time to undertake a praiseworthy action. Hopes fulfilled. Goodness of heart. Gifts, gratification, abundance, prosperity. Material wealth and to spare.

Reversed (or Negative): Desire, jealousy, envy, illusion. Possible loss. Unhappiness, fretfulness.

SEVEN OF COINS

The Seven of Coins is a card of profit, specifically of reaping the rewards of your labors.

Meaning

This is a card of profit—specifically of reaping the rewards of your labors. The profit is usually financial (given the suit!), but may be in any area in which the querent has worked long and well. It also predicts continued gradual growth, both personally and in business, with attending satisfaction in your work and its fruit. (In numerical sequence the card also suggests that at least part of the reason for your success is because of good deeds performed earlier; the result is or will be paid in good will toward the querent.)

In the Reading

Upright (or Positive): Success, usually financial. Gain in business or other enterprises. Profit, gain, money. Rewards for and satisfaction in work done. Gradual growth of the enterprise. Good fortune. Good will, by and toward the querent.

Reversed (or Negative): Money worries; specifically regarding an unwise expenditure or a loan the querent has been asked to make and which is not sure to be repaid. Your anxiety is well-founded; be careful here. Possible bad loans, heavy losses by gambling, bad luck.

EIGHT OF COINS

❧

The Eight of Coins says you know where you're going now, and how to get there, whether or not you realize it.

❧

Meaning

Once again, craftsmanship and knowledge is the key to eventual success, but here the success is closer. The Eight states that you know where you're going now, and how to get there; whether or not you realize it, you have the skills you need and need only employ them. Here success is based on your own personal training and experience; you've fairly and wisely earned the status you have or will soon attain.

In the Reading

Upright (or Positive): Understanding gained through experience; sureness of purpose. Employment, commissions, new business; practiced skills paying off and new skills developing. Craftsmanship. Your work will be well rewarded.

Reversed (or Negative): The querent is unsure what direction to go in, or even has not identified his or her ambitions; possible lack of ambition. Skill is also described here, but in the sense of someone being too clever for their own good; the mind turned to cunning and intrigue. Also, vanity, greed, false flattery, hypocrisy.

NINE OF COINS

ᶘᶅ

The Nine of Coins signifies order, security in possessions and relationships, the wisdom and experience you need to handle problems.

ᶘᶅ

Meaning

The Nine of Coins signifies order, security in possessions and relationships, accomplishment and success. Unlike the Three of Coins, which carried with it the suggestion that it was not the place to stop striving, the Nine is what success leads to and feels like. You have the wisdom and experience you need to properly manage your affairs and to handle any problems that may come up in the future. Your goals are well and truly accomplished, or soon will be.

In the Reading

Upright (or Positive): Order and discipline. Plenty in all things; material well-being. The ability to plan. Safety, security, prudence, success, accomplishment, wisdom. Freedom from want. Sometimes, recreation or a well-earned vacation.

Reversed (or Negative): Bad faith, deception, trickery, deceit. Plans voided or gone astray.

TEN OF COINS

✥

The Ten of Coins signifies you are established in both family and business, well-deserved feelings of confidence, possible inheritances.

✥

Meaning

This takes the prediction described in Nine one step further. You are established, in both family and business; what you worked for is now in your hands. The card also describes well-deserved feelings of confidence on the part of the querent, as well as well-earned honors received. Ten also carries with it the possibility of inheritances and legacies.

In the Reading

Upright (or Positive): Established family and business. Confidence and security, gain, honor. Emphasis on family matters; with business established, there is time for personal affairs. Inheritances, gifts, pension, wealth.

Reversed (or Negative): Chance, uncertainty, loss. Possible fatality. Robbery, gambling, hazards. Do not depend on your luck; it will change like the weather.

Wands

THE SUIT OF WANDS

Fourth, and last, in the line of precedence of the suits of the Minor Arcana, Wands in its own way promises the greatest glory.

In a reading, this suit usually refers to the querent's business or financial affairs, but not in the same way as Coins. Wands describes the potential, ambition, and personal effort which leads to success.

Wands originally represented the peasant or serf class in medieval society; the least influential and most powerless class on the social scale. A peasant had a limited amount of personal freedom, but his life could still be disrupted at will by any member of a higher class, and he could never hope to rise. There was a strict demarcation between classes which was not merely enforced by the upper classes, but also accepted by the lower classes.

Serfs were slaves. They were bound to the land on which they were born; no serf could set foot off his manor without the express permission of the manor lord.

A serf was required to perform services on demand and without compensation, and in addition owed to the lord of the manor a share of whatever he did earn or produce. Even his—or her—body belonged to the manor lord, to be used or disposed of as the serf's master wished.

On the other hand, serfs also had certain entitlements. A serf was legally entitled to the protection of his lord, and to assistance, financial, medical, or otherwise, if circumstances required it. In most cases, the serf was also legally entitled to his holding (the plot of land he worked, or whatever other job he performed), and could not be arbitrarily dispossessed. Serfs would also be cared for by their manor lord if they could not work for such reasons as age, infirmity, or sometimes even laziness. In fact, while the serf had no personal freedom, he or she did have a certain measure of personal security that was possible to no other class in medieval society, including the nobility.

So, there were two dangers in running away from your manor. There was the danger that you might be caught and punished, and there was the insecurity of having to try to make it on your own. For a serf to strike for freedom took not only physical courage, but a type of personal initiative which those who are born slaves usually lack.

Translated into modern terms, Wands describes anyone who started out (in our current sociological jargon) "disadvantaged"—poor, belonging to some group which is discriminated against, or handicapped in some way—but who overcame those disadvantages to achieve notable success. On a personal level, Wands describes the self-made man or woman: those who pulled themselves up by their own bootstraps, with little or no assistance and perhaps even against active opposition. Wands people also tend to be sympathetic to the struggles of others who are also trying to work their way up. They understand what you're going through, and are willing to offer advice and assistance. Unlike Cups people, if someone from the suit of Wands is on your side, their advice is always worth taking; it's not based on blind love, but on personal experience. Especially when it comes to advice on how to succeed, these are people who know what they're talking about.

People represented by Wands are those with personal initiative, especially anyone who started out at the bottom of the heap and succeeded against all odds to attain a position of wealth and honor. A Wands person will be intelligent, personally gifted, ambitious, and hardworking. This is also someone who can be trusted implicitly to do exactly what he or she says they will do—either good or bad, and either for against some other person.

It is important to note, in this context, that a Wands person has not only the will but the know-how to achieve his or her ends.

Another commonly accepted description of Wands people is that in at least some (not all!) cases their behavior tends to be *nouveau riche*: flamboyant in dress, displaying a love of luxury, and a tendency to show off what they've accomplished. Most such interpretations add that any criticism of this behavior is likely to come from people whose status was inherited rather than earned.

Those Wands people who do indulge in display are simply capable of enjoying what they've accomplished; in effect, having worked hard to achieve their success, they are generous with themselves as well as others.

Events or situations described by Wands are those involving the potential for success. Wands in a reading indicate the ability or opportunity, on the part of the querent, to achieve despite obstacles; or, they describe someone or some set of circumstances that favors the querent and will be helpful in some way. They also indicate a certain amount of just plain good luck: circumstances and events will work in your favor; opportunities will arise when you can recognize and are ready for them. And here note that while the interpretations of most of the cards refer to business or finance, your "business" can be any endeavor in which you are trying to succeed, whether or not it involves the making of money.

If a Wands card describes the querent, then he or she has the qualities of this suit, and can depend on their own experience, knowledge, and instincts in the situation being described. This is someone who either has succeeded or can succeed on their own initiative. If the querent is just starting out, then you're looking at success in embryo, and you can assure him or her that whatever goals they've set for themselves, they will eventually make it in a big way. In addition, the querent described by Wands is either a nice person to begin with or will become a nicer person as a result of his or her success.

As Swords and Cups are sister suits, so are Coins and Wands. Coins is the suit of wealth; Wands is the suit of personal achievement. In its own way, this suit also describes enterprise and worldly glory, and usually indicates financial success as well. But Wands carries with it the concept of fulfilling your potential to its fullest extent. Whether or not that fulfillment will also bring with it financial rewards depends on the circumstances, but the real reward promised by this suit is personal success in whatever terms you define it.

Description of the Suit Symbol

The depictions of Wands vary widely from deck to deck, and also, more than in any other suit, tend to be mixed within a single deck. In some cases, the wands are rods; finished and turned, with decorative or rounded ends. In others, they are wooden staffs, obviously cut from living wood and with leaves and/or flowers growing from at least one end. In still others, the wands are clubs, heavy, crudely trimmed, (baseball) bat-shaped, thicker at the striking end, and tapering to a narrower gripping end. This third depiction is often combined with one of the other two; for example, in a suit showing either rods or staffs, the ace may be a club, as well as the symbol carried by the Knight.

In decks which show the wands as staffs, the symbolism is of continued growth; in those which show finished rods the symbolism is of success achieved. The heavy clubs are probably symbolic of both the coarseness of this person's roots and the willingness to fight for position. Any of the three interpretations, or a combination of them, gives the allegory inherent in this suit: achievement accomplished and self-earned.

The Royal Court

Wands allegorizes financial or business success, personal initiative, and sometimes just plain good luck.

KING OF WANDS

The King of Wands is a man of status and wealth, or the time has come to take action in business matters.

Description

In most decks, the King of Wands is shown as a distinguished and dignified-looking man, seated on a throne. He may or may not be crowned or wearing armor: some decks show him dressed as a king; in others he appears as a prosperous merchant. He is obviously confident and at ease with himself and his position. His wand is a full-length staff or rod (nearly as tall as he would be if he were standing), and he holds it either leaning against his shoulder, or held out before him. Either way, its full length is clearly visible to the viewer. This is a man who is both proud of himself and sure of his position.

Meaning

When the King of Wands appears in the reading, he should call to mind a man of status and wealth who excels in the areas of business and finance. He is generally a man of humble origin who has succeeded either due to a stroke of good luck or, most often, because of his own intelligence and determination. He is likely to be someone whom the querent admires for both his position and his accomplishments. He is also someone who deserves this admiration: his word is good, and his advice can be trusted. If the querent is a man, the King may represent a rival, but a generous and honest one. If the querent is a woman, this man is either a relative or close family friend, but always a good advisor.

If this card does not describe a person, it indicates that the situation is favorable, or at least fair, to the querent, and that the time is probably auspicious to take action in business or financial matters.

In the Reading

Upright (or Positive): A man of status and wealth who is friendly toward the querent and willing to assist with either money or advice. He is honest, conscientious, and intelligent. If he is a rival, he will be a fair and generous one. If a friend, you are well-advised to take this man's advice. If not a person, the situation itself is an honest one: things are as they appear to be. Also, the possibility of unexpected good news, concerning an inheritance, a career advance, success in an ongoing or upcoming (usually business or financial) venture. Unexpected help or advice which will make your venture easier.

Reversed (or Negative): A man of authority and wealth who is austere but tolerant. He will not go out of his way to help you, but will not unnecessarily block you either, and he will approve efforts you make on your own. If not a person: you will have to work hard to achieve success, but circumstances are generally favorable at this time. You may not get much help, but there is nothing out there trying to stop you.

QUEEN OF WANDS

❧

The Queen of Wands represents an honorable, intelligent, friendly woman, confidante, or valuable assistance.

❧

Description

Many decks show the queen standing, holding the wand in her right hand, straight upward with one end resting on the ground. In some decks, she is seated on a throne. In either case, the wand is taller than she is. She may or may not be crowned; it depends on whether the deck depicts her as a queen or simply as a well-dressed woman. In many decks, the Queen also holds some other symbol in her left hand; sometimes a short scepter or scroll, sometimes a large flower (often a sunflower). Like the King, she is relaxed and at ease with herself and her position.

Meaning

The Queen of Wands should call to mind a woman of money and property. Both in the original interpretations and especially in our own times, it is highly possible that she owns or earned that financial standing herself, rather than simply riding on her husband's coattails. She is generally someone who displays a love of luxury; she dresses well and enjoys owning material things.

She can be generous and loving, but while her personality tends to be more magnetic than that of the King, she also tends to be more careful about the people she is willing to help or even to love. She is as sensible—and practical—in personal relationships as in business. She will expect value received for value given; love received for love given: almost a marketplace standard. However, when she gives her love, it will be sincere. If the querent is a man, this woman may represent his wife, or the woman he should marry (especially if he intends to succeed financially and needs someone to carry her share of the burden). If the querent is a woman, the Queen represents a long-time confidante and friend.

If this card represents a situation, then the time is right to initiate a new enterprise, especially one dealing with finances. You can expect help and advice along your way, and people who will assist you, and whose assistance will be valuable. This card can also indicate that you have the qualities within yourself that you need to succeed in your endeavor.

In the Reading

Upright (or Positive): An honorable, friendly, and intelligent woman. Displays a love of luxury. Sympathetic toward the querent and someone willing to help with either money or advice or both. A businesswoman or a woman of property; one who knows how to manage her money to the advantage of herself and her family. Economical, serious, a good counselor. A good time to make your move in an important endeavor, especially one involving business or finance.

Reversed (or Negative): A dangerous enemy, since she operates on intelligence more than emotion in her opposition. Especially dangerous if her own position, business, or family are threatened. If not a person, a time to be cautious, especially in important relationships (business or otherwise); don't step on any toes if you can avoid it. Deceit, infidelity, jealousy. Greed and avarice.

KNIGHT OF WANDS

❧

The Knight of Wands is a trustworthy, faithful young man, or a journey or move, change of job or relationship.

❧

KNIGHT ᴏғ WANDS.

Description

Most decks show a young man on a rearing or charging horse. In some decks, he is holding the wand as a weapon (and many decks which show the wand as a finished rod may show it here as a club), and is either attacking or warding off an enemy. In other decks, his position indicates that he is showing off more than charging; and in some, he appears to be admiring the wand or club he holds.

Meaning

If this card represents a person, it will be a young man whom the querent sees as a helpful relative or friend. As before, this individual has the same qualities as his symbolic parents; he is trustworthy, unselfish, and faithful; someone who will give up something for you. If this card does not represent a person, it generally indicates a journey or a move of some kind; a change of residence, change of job, or change in personal relationships.

In the Reading

Upright (or Positive): A male friend or relative who is willing to help the querent. He is a young man but mature in his behavior, and one who has an almost instinctive understanding of business and financial affairs, which is he is working to augment with training and experience. Also, an unselfish friend. In any case, someone whose advice you can trust and whose help you can take if you are in doubt. A journey, a change of residence or situation.

Reversed (or Negative): Arguments, discord in personal relationships. Breakup of a friendship; separation, or flight.

PAGE OF WANDS.

PAGE OF WANDS

The Page of Wands indicates a message is coming from a young friend, or information that will affect your current enterprise.

Description

Most decks show a young man standing in a country setting, leaning on a wand or staff. Also in most decks the staff is taller than he is. Usually his attitude is casual; he holds the wand with one hand at his side, and his position is relaxed. In some decks he holds the wand with both hands out in front of him. In almost all decks (except those which show the wand as a shorter club), he is looking at the top of the staff. The Page is well-dressed and wearing clothes similar to those of the King and Queen.

Meaning

The Page of Wands may represent either a young man or young woman, but with the same qualities as the King and Queen. He or she is likely to be sensitive in nature, but faithful. The appearance of this card in the reading indicates that you can expect some kind of news or message. If the card represents a person, the news will come from a young friend or relative; otherwise, it will just be information or an event that will strongly affect your current enterprise. The possibility also exists (if the card is reversed, or in an unfavorable reading) that this individual could be a rival.

In the Reading

Upright (or Positive): Possible help, or at least moral support, from a sensitive young friend or relative. Also, if you need someone to bear testimony in your favor (either in business or in family matters), this person will do so, or may have already done so. A faithful friend, a lover. Expect a message. A possible contract likely to be favorable.

Reversed (or Negative): If a person, this is someone who wants what you have or want, and who therefore cannot be trusted. A dangerous rival. Bad news. Instability and indecision. Flattery, which may put you off your guard.

The Pip Cards

The following ten cards are the number cards, or Pip Cards.

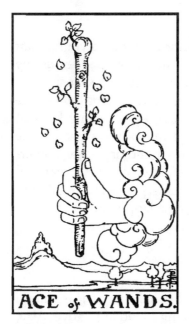

ACE OF WANDS

*The Ace of Wands
signifies
beginnings, possibly
an inheritance,
feelings of
contentment or
triumph.*

Description

Almost all decks, including those which show no art-work on the Aces of other suits, show a hand holding the wand or club at its base. In some decks, this hand is issuing from a cloud. Also in almost all decks, including the ones where the wands are finished rods, the Ace is club-shaped, or at the least has a heavier knob on one end; the symbolism being determination and willingness to fight if necessary. Note also almost all decks show leaves and branches growing out of the club, or somehow symbolized in the picture (such as floating alongside). The symbolism here is of new growth, despite, or perhaps because of, being cut off from its roots.

Meaning

The beginning of an enterprise, most probably involving business or finance. Creation, invention, and/or the source of these. A birth, usually of a business or an idea. Possibly an inheritance, which may be either of money or property, or of the ability needed to make the enterprise begun successful. The querent's state of mind is also appropriate; some decks read this card as feelings of contentment and triumph. This interpretation is similar to that of the Ace of Swords, but in a more positive sense. The implication here is not conquest or the defeat of enemies but rather of bonds broken and restraints put aside, enabling you to make your start; in effect, an escape to freedom.

In the Reading

Upright (or Positive): An auspicious start of a new business or enterprise. Also a good time to start. The circumstances are right, and the ideas and planning are also right. A state of contentment and triumph.

Reversed (or Negative): Ruin and decline. The project begun was either ill-conceived or else you did not have enough information or ability to do it, or the time was wrong. The other possibility is that your state of mind is less than appropriate. The reading, for example, may show that you could or should do this, but that you lack sufficient confidence or belief in yourself and/or in your enterprise. The result in any case will be failure unless the proper steps are taken.

TWO OF WANDS

~~~

The Two of Wands portends something unexpected will happen or enter the picture, or loss or failure in your new enterprise.

~~~

Meaning

The Two of Wands is not an auspicious card. Something unexpected is going to happen or enter into the picture. It is something you did not or could not allow for in your plans. At the least, it will catch you by surprise. But it could mean a loss or failure in your new enterprise.

Note that some interpretations reverse this meaning entirely and claim for the Two of Wands wealth, ownership, fortune, and magnificence. But most of these include the statement that there will be unhappiness along with it.

In the Reading

Upright (or Positive): Unforeseen problems with your new enterprise. Obstacles and opposition, possibly from the very people you were counting on for support. Possibilities include loss of money, failure of a marriage or partnership, general unhappiness or discontent with the way things are going or with the new business itself. Chagrin; an apparent success that turned sour.

Reversed (or Negative): Surprise, wonder, strong feelings evoked. You're in for a surprise of some kind. Whether it's a good or bad one will be revealed by surrounding cards. It's most likely to bring you trouble.

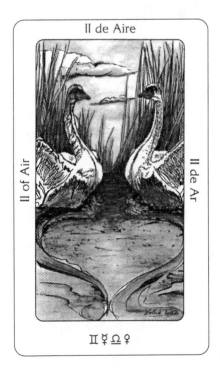

III de Aire

III of Air

III de Ar

THREE OF WANDS

The Three of Wands indicates problems can be resolved if the person remains calm, dignified, intelligent.

Meaning

The Three of Wands indicates problems can be resolved if the person in question remains calm and operates in a dignified, intelligent, and mature manner. Whatever problems were introduced earlier on can be overcome by the querent. Don't act impulsively; you know what to do. Use your experience and common sense.

In effect, if your earlier troubles were caused by your own mistakes or even your own feelings of inadequacy, acting in a mature and responsible manner will resolve them. If your problems were caused by the interference or opposition of others, you can still resolve them by taking things firmly in hand at this time. You may also expect people other than those who caused your problems to step in and help or advise you.

In the Reading

Upright (or Positive): A dignified approach to your business or enterprise will result in financial gain. You may also get help from an advisor or business associate. The card indicates cooperation as well as maturity as the key to successful action. More generally: success in business or trade; negotiations. A solid foundation can be or has been established.

Reversed (or Negative): Your problems resolved; the trouble you were having in this situation is over. You can expect either the end, or at least a suspension of, arguments and adversity. It should be fairly smooth sailing for a while.

FOUR OF WANDS

The Four of Wands shows you are out of trouble; relax and enjoy life for a while.

Meaning

Almost a sense of relief: you had some sticky times for a bit and then your troubles were suddenly resolved. Now you feel like it's time to relax and enjoy your life for a while. This card generally indicates happiness, harmony in business and personal partnerships, and enjoyable social activities.

In the Reading

Upright (or Positive): Enjoyment and gaiety. The pleasures money can buy; a material outlook on life; spending money you have on things you want. Harmony with others around you; a general situation of prosperity and comfort.

Reversed (or Negative): Almost the same meaning, but possibly less flamboyantly (and less expensively) expressed. Personal satisfaction in a job well done. Prosperity. Adding to your property or business.

FIVE OF WANDS

᭩᭢

The Five of Wands signifies greed, competition for financial gain, hardship.

᭢᭩

Meaning

As follows from a period of wild spending and less than mature financial handling, you are spending most of your time trying to figure out how to win or earn or get more money and material things. This is not simply a matter of trying to make your business grow; it is greedy competition for material gain. Expect hardship for a time, based on this hand-to-hand struggle. If you're doing this yourself, you may be able to ease your situation by easing off. If it's caused by other people, you will have to fight them to keep what you have.

[Note: Some interpretations call this the card of gold, gain, or wealth. You may get the riches you're after if other signs are favorable.]

In the Reading

Upright (or Positive): Greed and competition for financial gain or material goods. "Keeping up with the Jones'"; a struggle for wealth and fortune. Hardship. Immature decisions or goals.

Reversed (or Negative): The competition is neither fair nor honest. Expect trickery, disputes, and even legal problems and litigation.

WANDS (6) WANDS

△ Victory △

SIX OF WANDS

The Six of Wands represents very good news, a message of hope and victory, may indicate gifts about to be received.

Meaning

Here again, the querent can expect something new to enter into the picture, but in this case, the news is good. Expect very good news, a message of hope and victory. Also may indicate gifts about to be received. In either case, something you've hoped for will come to pass.

In the Reading

Upright (or Positive): Good news is on the way. A hope will be fulfilled or desires gratified. Gifts received. You've made, or are about to make, a significant conquest; you will win some issue. You've carried your affairs to a successful point and are about to receive your rewards and recognition for your efforts.

Reversed (or Negative): Delays, most possibly caused by treachery. Your fears are justified. Prepare for battle: the enemy is at the gate. Disloyalty, infidelity, obstacles that may overcome or defeat your enterprise.

SIX OF SPEARS

THE RETURN
OF AMBROSIUS

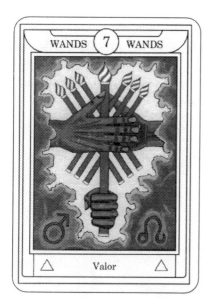

WANDS 7 WANDS

Valor

SEVEN OF WANDS

The Seven of Wands foretells success achieved by courage and determination, profit and gain.

Meaning

The Seven of Wands is a foreteller of success achieved by courage and determination. The indications are of profit and gain; some interpretations call this card "the treasury symbol." You have faced off your competition and will emerge the victor. If this card comes up in answer to a question, it can also indicate a good time to take a risky gamble; again, especially one involving money.

In the Reading

Upright (or Positive): Financial gain. Success. At least one major part of your enterprise achieved. There will be competition and strife, but if you stand your ground you can stand off your enemies. Even though it may look as though you're outnumbered, you have the advantage.

Reversed (or Negative): Consider this a warning not to hesitate. Make up your mind now, and take action. You're confused as to what moves to make, but the situation is such that even the wrong action, if taken decisively, will be better than doing nothing at all. This is not the time for uncertainty or indecision.

VIII de Aire

VIII of Air

VIII de Ar

♀♄

EIGHT OF WANDS

The Eight of Wands says this is a time to take action, to be hopeful, to plan your next moves.

Meaning

Make speed toward your goals; this is your moment. You're on the road to almost assured success. Don't be precipitate, just active. It is also a time for planning your next moves from here.

Be prepared not just for the single upcoming event(s) but what will follow from them. Things are going to start to move now. Note that though this suit usually concerns business and finance, this card can also indicate arousal of love; though love in this case may be either between people or love for your work.

In the Reading

Upright (or Positive): A time to take action; to start on the next phase of your enterprise. A time to be hopeful, and to make haste. Things are on the move; move with them. Also: good luck, arousal of love.

Reversed (or Negative): Quarrels, jealousy, internal disputes (as between spouses, business partners, etc.), opposition. Things are still moving, but either the situation or the consequences or both can be unpleasant to go through. Again, be prepared; know exactly what you're doing. The times are right not just for you but for others, and that means somebody is likely to get hurt in the free-for-all.

NINE OF WANDS

❧❧❧

The Nine of Wands represents a job well-done, the ability to plan wisely, courage under fire.

❧❧❧

Meaning

The task is performed successfully; the job is done. The person to whom this card refers has learned discipline, the ability to plan wisely, and courage under fire. Even if there are problems (which may be shown by other cards in the reading), you know how to deal with them; they no longer defeat you just by happening. If there is opposition, your skills, strength, and courage will make you a formidable opponent.

In the Reading

Upright (or Positive): Strength, boldness. Ability to deal with problems or delays. Strong opposition to wrongs. Self-discipline, order. Final success in your endeavors.

Reversed (or Negative): Failure, calamity. The possibility that you have learned nothing from all your efforts; your success injured or stalled due to your own obstinacy. Loss of money; disputes among friends or partners. Obstacles and delay. Expect the worst.

WANDS (10) WANDS

Oppression

Ten of Wands

The Ten of Wands represents the feeling you can do anything, but also warns not to take things for granted.

Meaning

The feeling that you can do anything, win at anything. This may encourage a gamble for high stakes, and such a gamble can result in great gain.

[Note: if surrounding cards are inimical, the gain may happen anyway, but will bring unhappiness and trouble.]

This card also contains a warning not to take things for granted; you have succeeded in your initial enterprise, but it puts you in a position to achieve greater things, and these things will be just as hard to achieve as the one you have just accomplished.

In the Reading

Upright (or Positive): Fortune, gain, success, but also possible unhappiness from these things. Possible uncertainties in your enterprise, but if you assert yourself, honor, security, opposition swept away.

Reversed (or Negative): Intrigues and difficulties. These may be legal (as a lawsuit), or between people. A great possibility of loss; if surrounding cards are negative, you may lose all you've gained. Treachery. Note: if this card is reversed but surrounding cards are positive, the negative influences are still there, but you will be able to ward them off. In that case, this card is a warning against trouble or false friends.

Divining with
the Tarot

Reading the Tarot

HOW TO TELL FORTUNES

There are many different systems used to read the Tarot cards, and there's no reason to suppose that one system is better than the rest. Some Tarot readers will use an alternate layout, or spread, for different kinds of circumstances; others settle on one spread that they find works best for them and use it all the time.

How you ultimately decide to lay out your cards is entirely up to you. As long as your system gets you answers, it's the best one for you to use.

This chapter gives you the basic procedure for doing a Tarot reading, with explanations, for both querent and reader, of how to get the most information from what the cards are trying to tell you. The next chapter describes three different Tarot spreads. Each spread includes a sample reading, done specifically for the

purpose of this book, as an illustration of how to interpret and correlate the meanings of the cards. Let's start
with some basic definitions.

There are two people involved in any Tarot reading—even one you do for yourself. The first is the person who lays out the cards and interprets their meaning
(variously called the Reader, the Diviner, or the Seer).
The second is the person for whom the reading is done
(the Querent, Consultant, or Questioner).

For both reader and querent, your purpose is to get
an understanding of a situation which is in progress or
about to happen. You're looking for information which
is not readily available by ordinary means. That information—if you play your cards right!—will be provided
by your divining tool, in this case, the Tarot deck.

As the reader, your first priority—before you even
take out your deck—is to make sure the querent understands what's going on.

If the querent is familiar with Tarot readings, there's
not much you need to explain up front. At most, and
only if you've never read for this person before, you will
need to tell him or her how you want them to handle the
cards; and, depending on the type of reading, how you
want them to phrase their question. You can explain how
your system works (the significance of individual cards
in your spread) as you are doing the reading.

If the querent has never had their cards read
before, then there's a great deal more you have to explain. You should begin by telling them what kinds of
questions the Tarot will—and won't —answer. One way
to do this is simply to say that the Tarot can reveal information about your past, present, and future, and/or
about people or situations you're involved with. But it

will not predict your state's lottery number—past, present, or future! Then make certain the querent understands these basic facts about how a Tarot reading works:

First: You can do a generalized reading (i.e., one in which no question is asked, just a description of what's happening in the querent's life at this time). But if there is a question, it must be phrased properly. *The more specific your question, the more specific and accurate your answer will be.*

Second: Whether or not you ask a question, the cards will tell you what you need to know. And that may not, necessarily, be what you want or hope to hear.

Third: The future is mutable. You don't get your fortune told to find out the inevitable; if that were the case, any divining operation would be pointless, and even depressing. The cards will tell you what is most likely to happen, given the current and past circumstances. If the question has been properly phrased, they will also tell you why these events are occurring or likely to occur, and suggest a possible course of action. It is then up to the querent to decide what steps he or she is prepared to take to either make sure this event does occur, or to prevent it.

Fourth: It can happen that the question you asked, no matter how well-phrased, is not the one that's answered. This is most likely to occur if the querent has never had their cards read before, or if it's been a long time since they've had them read. I call it "We interrupt this program for an important announcement." What happens in this case is that the cards ignore the question that was asked, and instead address an entirely different situation. In all cases where I've seen this happen, the question that was answered instead was of much more vital importance to the querent. It's almost as if Something had been trying to get through to this person and grasped the opportunity of a Tarot reading as a means of communication.

Should this happen, complete the reading anyway, giving the querent as much information as you can. Then, if your querent still wants their initial question answered (and there have been times when people have been too shaken up to ask!), you can do a second reading. In that second reading, you will generally get the answer to their first question.

Finally: Sometimes you won't get an answer to your question at all. Assuming the reader is not having an off-day (and no one can be clairvoyant all the time!), there are generally two reasons why the cards won't answer. The first reason is because the question was not specific enough. The old axiom "If you want to find an answer, first you have to know the question" certainly applies to Tarot readings. If you think this might be the problem, simply rephrase the question and try again. Over time, you will learn how questions should be worded to elicit the best information.

Another reason the cards won't answer is because the querent is not supposed to know the answer at this time. There are some situations that people have to take on trust. And there are also times when it is unwise or even dangerous for someone to know in advance what the outcome of a given situation will be. The answers you get from the Tarot cards will be whatever information is currently available to the querent—and that means information the querent is allowed to know.

If the cards refuse to answer, you can try again at a later date; say, in a few days or a week. By that time the situation may have changed just enough that the Tarot will be willing to give you at least a hint of what's going on.

There is also a third reason an answer may be confusing or entirely off-base—or seem to be. This generally happens in a reading that you do for yourself, though it can also happen when you read for someone you know very well.

In this case, it's very likely that you are getting an accurate answer, but that you're simply not "listening." Tarot readers are human too—and like everyone else have a tendency to make snap judgements or draw conclusions that are not based on either the facts or their own intuitive abilities. When you know, or think you know, too much about the situation or the querent, there is a tendency to make assumptions, or to read things into the cards that simply aren't there. This is the primary reason that the hardest reading to do is one you do for yourself,

That doesn't mean you can't learn to read for yourself, however. After all, if you're putting this much work into learning the cards, it's only fair that you should be able to make direct personal use out of what you've learned! In order to read for yourself, or a close friend, you have to learn to separate reader and querent—in effect, to "disconnect" your conscious, decision-making faculties and let the cards lead you where they will.

Remind yourself that the reason you're using the cards in the first place, rather than making a decision on your own, is because you want an independent judgement of the situation. Simply interpret the cards as you see them and accept what they tell you as though you were being told by someone else.

Now let's review the procedure for doing a Tarot reading. No matter what kind of system you use, for almost all readings the first card you will lay out on the table is the one which Tarot readers call the *Significator*.

Choosing the Significator

The basic concept behind the Tarot is that each individual is the center of his or her own microcosm. So when you do a reading, you place the querent at the center of the spread. Before you shuffle, go through the deck and choose a card to represent the querent (or, if the question calls for it, which describes some other person, or the nature of the situation about which the question is being asked). This card is called the Significator.

There are a number of ways to choose a Significator. For a Significator that represents the querent, some readers use one of two cards from the Major Arcana: the Magician if the querent is a man, or the High Priestess if the querent is a woman. This expresses the querent as the central, or controlling, factor in the situation under discussion.

If you prefer to use a Significator which specifically describes your querent (or if the question is about some other person), you can use one of the court cards from the Minor Arcana.

You begin by selecting a card that describes the individual's age and sex. The choices here are standard. If the querent is a man forty years old or older, use a King. If he is less than forty, use a Knight. If the querent is a woman of forty or older, use a Queen; for a younger woman, use the Page. The Page may also be used for teenagers or children.

You have more leeway in your choice of a suit, but also more of a decision to make. You want to choose the suit that best describes this individual's personal characteristics.

If you know, or have a feeling, about what kind of person you're dealing with, choose the suit which in your judgement best represents the querent's character. Next best would be to base your choice on his or her emotional state or attitude in this situation; or, you can select a suit to represent the querent's primary concern. And finally, you can simply choose a suit which describes the querent's physical appearance.

Note that you choose your suit to meet only *one* of these criteria: don't try to match all of them. For example: an energetic person should be represented by Swords, even if he or she is fair in coloring. Someone whose primary concern involves business or profession should be represented by Wands, even if their hair is black and their skin is dark. Basing your choice on physical appearance is a last resort in any case; it's always best to select on the basis of character traits if you can.

Here are the traditional guidelines for selecting the most representative card. Because this particular sequence makes the descriptions easier to remember, I've arranged the order of the suits from lightest coloring to darkest:

WANDS (Air)

Physical Appearance: People with very light coloring. This includes those with blond or light auburn hair, very fair skin, and blue eyes.

Character or Emotional State: A self-made or ambitious person. A generous person, or one concerned about or willing to help others. A successful, self-assured, or confident person. Also, a flashy dresser.

Primary Concern: If the question involves career choices or abilities, personal ambition, or the probabilities of success in some venture.

CUPS (Water)

Physical Appearance: For someone slightly darker in coloring. A person with blue or gray eyes and light brown or dull blond hair. Skin may still be fair, but tans rather than burns.

Character or Emotional State: A loving or affectionate person. Someone who avoids arguments, tries to make peace whenever possible. Someone "laid-back," lethargic, even lazy. Good-natured, good-tempered, happy, pleasant or kind.

Primary Concern: If the question involves the querent's emotional life or emotional state. Any situation where the key to a solution is how the querent feels, or should feel, about people or events involved. Includes spiritual issues.

SWORDS (Fire)

Physical Appearance: People with dark brown hair and hazel or gray eyes, who have a dull, or darker complexion or skin tone.

Character or Emotional State: A dominant or a domineering person. Someone who is strong, healthy, and/or energetic. Someone who is physically brave. Someone impatient, angry, vindictive, or contentious (even if only in this situation). Also, someone who is cold or uncaring.

Primary Concern: If the question involves mental or intellectual state. If the question involves decisions to be made, especially if those decisions require clear-thinking and lack of emotional entanglements. Note: Use this suit to represent enemies only if the Significator is chosen to represent the querent's enemy rather than the querent. Otherwise see below: Major Arcana

COINS (Earth)

Physical Appearance: People darkest in coloring. Those with dark-brown or black hair, dark eyes, and sallow, swarthy, or dark complexions.

Character or Emotional State: An earthy person. Unspiritual; very worldly-minded. Money or material minded; very rich or having money troubles. Also; someone who is well-dressed.

Primary Concern: If the question involves physical or material status, money matters, or questions of property or inheritance.

Keep in mind that these descriptions are only guidelines which you can use until you become more familiar with the cards, and more adept at doing readings. You will eventually get to the point where you *know* which card represents the querent; you'll be able to assess the person for whom you're doing a reading and pick a Significator on feel. But even as a beginner, if you have a feeling about which card would make the best Significator, then use it, no matter how it may contradict these definitions, and even if you can't explain to yourself or anyone else why you chose it.

For some readings, it's better to use as your Significator a card that describes the situation or the question. In that case, choose your card from the Major Arcana, based on which trump card best illustrates the circumstances. For example, if the situation involves matters of law, or the basis of the question is whether or not justice will be served (though not necessarily whether or not your querent will win!), choose the Justice card as the Significator. If your querent is involved in an uphill struggle of some kind, or is faced with enemies or opposition, and wants to know how or if he or she will be able to handle it, choose the Strength card. Use your best judgement as to how the basic interpretations of the cards fit the situation.

Finally: sometimes the Significator will be chosen for you. In some readings, you may find that while the question is being answered, the final, or outcome, card is inconclusive or puzzling. If that is the case, use that card as your Significator when you do a second reading to clarify the answer.

Dealing the Cards

Once you've chosen the Significator, the cards must be shuffled and cut for the reading. The basic method for doing this is fairly simple. Different readers, however, add their own variations, and in each case for some very good reasons.

To try to include all, or even most of those variations here would result in a convoluted and unnecessarily confusing dissertation (I know, because I did try). What I've done instead is simply give you the basic method as a starting point. But should you find, or invent, any embellishment to this method that makes it work better for you, by all means use it. As with everything else, the definition of the best way to prepare your deck is simple: use whatever method consistently results in accurate readings. That said, here's how you shuffle and cut:

Keep the deck face down throughout.

With the Significator removed from the deck, the cards should be thoroughly shuffled by the reader. This serves two purposes: it insures that the cards are well mixed, and it "clears" the deck of any influences that may have remained from prior readings. When you shuffle, don't try to keep all the cards facing in one direction. Remember that a card which comes up reversed, or upside down, in the layout can change its meaning.

Next, the querent should ask his or her question. (If this is a general reading, you can skip this step.) The question should be formulated as clearly and precisely as possible, and stated aloud.

If the querent has trouble formulating a question, then ask him or her to explain the problem, until you have enough details for you to suggest how the question should be phrased. Try not to elicit too much information: you want to get your answers from the Tarot cards, not from your own preconceived ideas of what must be the case.

With the question in mind, the cards are now shuffled for the reading. Shuffle at least three times; more if you feel the need (or until the deck "feels right"). This may be done by either the querent or the reader, depending on your preference. Note, however, if you choose to shuffle the cards yourself, it should not be because a given querent doesn't know how to handle a deck of cards. *The order in which the cards come up during a reading is not accidental.* No matter who shuffles or how poorly, the cards you deal into your spread will be the right ones for that reading.

After shuffling, the deck must be cut. No matter who shuffled, this operation should be performed by the querent. The usual procedure is to cut the deck twice, into three stacks; it doesn't matter whether or not the stacks are even.

You'll find that many books on the Tarot specify that the deck be cut with the left hand. The reasoning here is that the right, or dominant, hand is more involved in conscious activities, and so the left hand is more attuned to the subconscious or psychic level. I've seen no comments on whether or not this means that a left-handed person should cut with their right hand. Even those readers who include this step in their instructions do agree that it is not essential to getting an accurate reading. Again, try it and see if it makes any difference in the results of your readings.

After the querent cuts the deck, the reader takes the three stacks and recombines them into one, in whatever order seems best at the time. Then you deal the cards in order from the top of the deck until you have enough to complete your spread. The rest of the deck will be put aside; it will not be used for this reading.

You can turn the cards face up one at a time as you interpret them, or you can turn them all up at once, to get a general impression of the major influences at work before you begin your interpretation. When you turn the cards up, don't "flip" them: turn them over from left to right, rather than bottom to top, so that they continue to face in their original direction. This is especially important if you are using upright and reverse in your reading.

[Note: It doesn't matter whether the querent is seated across from you, or next to you; the relative position of any card in the reading depends on where you are sitting. The cards are always read as they face the reader.]

Doing the Reading

And now that you finally have your cards spread out for a reading, here are some basic guidelines for determining what they're trying to tell you.

First: In a reading, each card is considered separately first, and then in relation to surrounding cards. The nature of those surrounding cards will alter the meaning of an individual card; either strengthen or diminish it, or help to clarify its intent.

For example (and please take into account that these are only generalizations. An actual interpretation would depend on which cards come up in a specific reading, and how they are positioned):

The King of any suit has a strong influence on the outcome of a situation. However, the influence of a King card can be either increased or diminished if the King of another suit appears in the same reading. The presence of the King of Wands, especially in a reading heavy with Wands and/or Coins, indicates that someone influential may be willing to help you on a professional level. If the King of Cups also appears, the indications are even stronger that someone is working in your favor, or is at the very least friendly toward you. But if the King of Swords appears, you have a powerful enemy. That enemy may be the King of Wands, or it may be someone else who will turn him against you.

What kind of situation is under discussion also clarifies the meaning of an individual card. For example, the Six of Wands predicts gifts received, a hope fulfilled. The question is, what is the nature of the gift? If surrounding cards are Coins, then expect money or property; if they are Wands, expect a promotion or career advancement. If surrounding cards are Cups, however, then the gift will have to do with love rather than money: look for flowers and candy—or an engagement ring.

The nature of the question should also affect the way you interpret the cards. For example, if the question is about love, then a material gain—even if predicted by Coins—refers to an improvement in the relationship. If the question involves someone's health, then that same card predicts healing. Money may, or may not, have an influence in both cases, but focus primarily on the circumstances described by the question.

And don't forget that the most important factor that will affect your interpretations is the querent. For example, if a reading predicts that the querent is going to receive money, where it will come from depends on that person's situation. For someone looking for work, it may mean they'll find a job; for someone with a job, it may mean a raise, promotion, or bonus. For someone in business, it may mean an increase in sales; for a student, it may mean financial assistance with tuition or a scholarship. Always adapt the conventional meanings of the cards so that they relate to the question, or the person for whom you're doing the reading.

Second: Once all the cards in your spread are face up, check to see if any one suit dominates the reading. If so, you have a *ruling suit*. This means that the type of circumstances described by that suit is of such vital importance in the querent's current situation that it will affect everything else he or she does or is involved in. If out of ten cards, for example, four or five of them are Cups and the others are divided among other suits (including the Major Arcana), then Cups is the ruling suit. It means that emotional issues are the key to the querent's current situation or question—even if the question is about career or money.

In the same respect, if a single card is flanked by two cards of the same suit (and especially if it is surrounded by them), then whatever may be the interpretation of that card, its influence will be tempered by the flanking suit; it will be ruled by that suit. Your interpretation of the individual card, or of the reading as a whole, must be tempered by the influence of ruling cards.

Here are the influences imposed on the reading by each suit if it is the ruling suit:

If the Major Arcana predominates in a reading, then it is the querent's own psychological or spiritual condition that will determine the outcome of the situation. The Major Arcana explains the personal changes or growth (or lack of growth!) the querent is going through which will affect either his or her outlook or the way he or she deals with the situation. In effect, the querent has control of everything that's happening or going to happen—if he or she can control themselves.

If the ruling suit comes from the Minor Arcana, and especially if it primarily involves court cards, then the primary influences come from outside, and may very well be circumstances over which the querent has no personal control.

If the ruling suit is Swords, then enemies, bad luck, or other adverse influences are hard at work, and good influences will find it much more difficult to operate. This is a very unpleasant and possibly dangerous situation; you are being warned that people and/or circumstances are working against you. Be very careful.

If Cups is the ruling suit, then emotional issues, such as love, friendship, or other strong and usually positive feelings influence the progress and outcome of the reading. In general, a preponderance of Cups also indicates that good will, toward the querent or in general, will modify the circumstances, strengthening good influences and softening adverse ones.

Coins dominating the reading indicate that practical matters, including those involving money and property, rule the progress of this situation. A predominance of cards from this suit does not necessarily mean that the querent is going to become very rich; it is more likely to indicate that success will be achieved or problems resolved only if money is available or can be obtained.

These cards also sometimes point to business or personal competition or friction over matters of money or property. In any event, for good or bad the reading is concerned with worldly matters and the influence or building of wealth.

Wands as the ruling suit may also indicate that business matters, especially those involving training, education, or career advancement, rule the situation. But for the most part, a preponderance of Wands indicates that friendship and/or influence will have the greatest effect on the outcome of the situation. With good cards, Wands mean that friends can help assure success; with bad ones that they may help to overcome problems. In any case, you're being advised not to go it alone, and that you don't have to. Rely on your friends and contacts—and keep them happy!

You should also look for a combination of "sister suits" as a possible *ruling influence* on the reading. A combination of Swords and Cups indicates that strong, and opposing, feelings are the key to the problem under discussion: love and hate, friendship and enmity, friends and foes will take a hand in things. If Coins and Wands combine to rule the reading, then money and business matters are the most important issue and must be resolved before you can go on to anything else.

Third: *Trust your own insights when interpreting the cards.*

The impressions you get, instinctively or clairvoyantly, while you're handling the cards must and should affect your interpretations. The Tarot is a means of freeing your unconscious psychic abilities. And the accuracy of any answer you get will depend more on your own skill and insight than on the cards themselves.

Some people are naturally clairvoyant and can automatically use the Tarot cards as a kind of channeling device to a higher level of consciousness. But even if your intuitive abilities are limited, or—in your opinion—missing altogether, the cards will help you develop the insights you need to forecast the future. Start by using intellectual observation: by making deductions based on the combinations of cards that come up in a reading, and on your personal experience with similar situations in your own life. In the beginning, you may feel like you're just guessing, and perhaps you will be. With time and practice, however, you will access the instincts you need to see clearly. A rule of thumb I've found to be true is this: if you truly had no psychic ability at all, you would also have no interest in learning how to read the Tarot. Just the fact that you've gotten this far proves that you have a gift for prophecy waiting to be developed.

Fourth: If you're really puzzled, very often the querent can help clarify the meaning of individual cards, or the reading as a whole. It's the querent's life that is under discussion after all; so he or she will be able to make an association that you would not be aware of. If the meaning of a card is unclear, give the querent the interpretation and ask what it means to him or her. It's not your purpose to astound or mystify (at least, I hope not!), but to help the querent get at the truth.

Fifth: You have to tell the truth as you find it in the reading. Yes; be as pleasant as you can in revealing the meaning of the cards. You're not doing this to frighten or upset anyone; so if you can emphasize the positive, then do so. But again, you are trying to help the querent get at the facts. So if a reading reveals an unpleasant set of circumstances in the works, you have to say so.

It can be very tempting, especially if a reading predicts some kind of disaster, to just ignore the cards and predict sweetness and light. But you do your querent no good by glossing over the facts. If you're really disturbed by what you see in a given spread, you can reshuffle and try again; it's always possible that a mistake was made somewhere along the line. But if the same type of prediction appears again, then make sure you tell the querent exactly what you see. The future can be changed by anyone willing to make the effort— but only if they have the facts.

Sixth: How many times should you repeat a reading? You will find people who ask you to re-read the cards over and over again at the same sitting. Sometimes it's because they have more than one question— but very often, the reason they want the cards read again is because they didn't like the answer they got the first time.

You can consult the cards as often as you need to. But in general, they should only be read two, or at the most three, times at one sitting for the same querent. If you are re-reading on the same question, your purpose should be only to clarify something that was unclear the first time. Otherwise, you're just wasting your time: you are not going to get the Tarot to "change its mind." Even if the querent has more than one question, there is still a limit as to how many readings you can do for the same person at one sitting. (For no other reason, you as the reader may find yourself getting impatient with this person, and that means your ability to interpret the cards is going to slip.) It's generally best to wait at least a week before repeating a reading. This is true even if repeat readings at the first sitting still didn't fully clarify an answer. When you re-read at that later date, interpret the cards in terms of recent events. The lag time gives the situation some time to change or develop.

Seventh: If the same card comes up in repeated readings, either at the same sitting or within a few days of the initial reading, it acquires additional importance—whether or not successive readings involve the same question. And both you and the querent must pay special attention to whatever person or set of circumstances the card describes.

Figure it out yourself. There are seventy-eight cards in the Tarot deck; and most spreads use only a small fraction of the cards. Even if you use the same basic layout every time you do a reading, there are literally millions of possible combinations that can come up. If you vary your spreads for different kinds of questions, the number of possible combinations increases. Assuming the cards have been well-shuffled, the statistical probability of the same card repeating itself is very low.

Obviously, then, if a given card does repeat, the situation or person it represents is going to have a significant impact on the course of events within the immediate future. A card that repeats in successive readings, and especially if it repeats more than once, acquires the status of a ruling card.

Finally: The divinatory meanings you've been given for the cards were expressed as "Upright or Positive" and "Reversed or Negative." Here's what it means:

When you deal out your spread, those cards which face the reader (i.e., which are right-side up from the reader's perspective) are upright; those which face away from the reader are reversed.

Each of the cards in the Tarot deck has both a positive and a negative interpretation. In most cases, it can seem that a positive interpretation means good things are going to happen, and a negative one means bad things are going to happen. But that's not true all the time. For a card like The Tower of Destruction, for example, the positive interpretation is absolute disaster. If the card is reversed—or, if the meaning is negated—you've still got problems, but they're not as serious. The positive interpretation of a card, then, is its strongest meaning; a negative interpretation results when the influence of the card has been weakened, delayed—or reversed.

The reason that the positive meanings of each card have been assigned to the upright position and the negative meanings to the reverse is because many Tarot readers feel that how a card comes up in a spread is not a random occurrence, but portends a change in the situation it reveals or affects. For those who do interpret the cards this way, it seems logical to assume that if a given card is dealt out reversed, that indicates that its meaning has also been reversed—or at least altered to some degree—as well.

However, you will also find interpretations for the cards that do not take into account their possible upright or reverse position in the spread. These readers feel that it is the nature of the situation at hand, or the influence of other cards in the reading, which strengthen or weaken the effect of any individual card. In this case, the reader decides the relative meaning of a card based on its association with surrounding cards and/or on the interpretation of the reading as a whole. (Most people who interpret the cards this way also turn all the cards in their spread upright, or facing the reader, before they begin their analysis.) As with everything else you've been told so far, there is no best way to decide this. You can use the upright or reverse position of a card as a clue to which part of the interpretation applies in any reading, or you can base your analysis conclusions solely on associations with other cards. Both systems have their advantages. Assuming an upright/reverse association makes it faster and easier to decide which set of meanings applies at the time of the reading. Assuming position is unimportant gives you that much more leeway in deciding which interpretations you will apply to the card. Again, try it both ways. *Whichever system you find works best for you is the one you should use!* And it will not, in the long run, adversely affect your ability to correctly interpret the cards. As long as you use the same system every time you do a reading, your deck will go along

with you. The cards have a way of arranging themselves in the order needed for the reading.

And now that you have all your instructions,
exceptions, and explanations, it's time you had a chance
to practice doing some actual readings. Let's take a look
at three different ways to lay out the Tarot cards.

THREE WAYS TO GET ANSWERS

Tarot spreads range from very simple to extremely complex. Most spreads don't use the entire deck; but there are some that use half the deck or more, just as there are some that can be completed with ten cards or less. Obviously, the more cards you need for your spread, the more complicated and time-consuming it will be to use—and to learn.

Even for experienced readers, simpler is often best. Fewer cards make the spread easier for the reader to interpret and the querent to understand. Less data to correlate also means less chance for errors in interpretation, so the smaller spreads can sometimes be more accurate. And in the long run, the information you get can be just as detailed as in more complex systems. For these reasons, all three spreads described in this chapter use a minimal number of cards.

Simple or complex, however, the explanations of what each of the cards in a spread is intended to show you can still be confusing if you've never done a reading before. An actual reading demonstrates, better than any explanation, how the cards relate to each other in a real-life situation, and how to understand their meanings in terms of surrounding cards and the question asked. So for each of the spreads described here, you will get a complete explanation of how it works, and then an example of how it did work.

The sample readings in this chapter were selected from a series of readings done for actual people, with the needs of this book in mind. I chose as samples those readings which best illustrate how the Tarot answers questions, the way you choose which interpretation applies, and how you need to adjust those interpretations within the context of the reading. However, even in a spread that uses a limited number of cards, very often the results can be complex. So from those "best illustrations," I also selected those three which were easiest to explain.

Because these sample readings are intended to illustrate how to interpret the combinations of cards in a reading, you'll be given a little bit more information than the reader would normally ask for. Explanations of the interpretations include the querent's perceptions and feedback as well; where applicable, I'll also tell you not just what the cards said, but what eventually happened to that person in the situation described.

No information which would reveal the identity of any querent is given. Each of the sample readings in this chapter are included with the permission of the person for whom they were done.

Now let's get started. Here are three ways to lay out your cards for a reading.

A Ten-Card Spread

One of the most commonly used Tarot spreads is called by most readers the Ancient Celtic Method. This spread uses just enough cards to give a fairly detailed picture of the querent's current circumstances. The Celtic spread can be used for a general reading; it is also one of the best spreads to use if you want an answer to a definite question.

Once the deck has been shuffled and cut, the Significator is placed face up in the center of the table. With the deck face down, take the first ten cards in order from the top of the deck and place them into the spread as described below (see Figure One).

The position of each card in this spread has a definite reference to a specific area of the querent's life or current circumstances.

FIRST CARD: *This covers you.* Take the first, or top, card of the deck and place it face up on top of the Significator. This card describes the basis of the situation or its present influences. It tells you the general atmosphere in which the querent is currently operating, including the querent's state of mind in this situation, and/or the people or other influences presently at work.

SECOND CARD: *This crosses you.* The second card is placed horizontally across the first. If you are using upright and reverse in your reading, the side facing the reader should be toward the right.

This card either strengthens or weakens the effects of the first card. It shows obstacles or ameliorating circumstances; events and situations which currently exist or are coming up in the immediate future, and which will have a direct effect on the situation in question. If it is a favorable card, then any good influences in the first card will be strengthened, any bad will be weakened. If it is an unfavorable card, it will weaken or cancel out any good influences in the first card, or increase the chances of bad influences.

THIRD CARD: *This crowns you.* The third card is placed above the Significator and first card. It describes the querent's goals in this matter, and the probability of achieving them at this time. Specifically, this card explains the querent's ideal aim (what he or she hopes to accomplish in this situation), and/or the best that can be achieved under the circumstances—whether or not it's what the querent wants. It also represents the immediate future, in that the situation described by this card has not yet occurred.

FOURTH CARD: *This is beneath you.* This card is placed below the Significator. It describes the foundation of the situation under discussion; a specific event or series of events in the immediate past which, because of their influence on the querent, are the reason, or direct cause, of the current situation.

[Note: By the time you've read these four cards, you will know what question your spread is answering. You've been told what the situation is about; what can either help or hurt the querent in these circumstances; what the querent wants; and what happened previously that got him or her into this situation in the first place. The querent will now be able to tell you if the cards are answering the question that was asked, or if they have decided to address another set of circumstances instead.]

FIFTH CARD: *This is behind you.* Place this card to the right of the Significator. It gives the influence or set

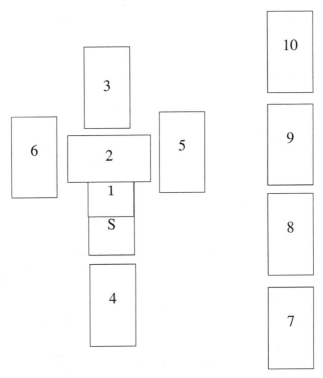

Figure One: Ten-Card Spread or Celtic Cross

of circumstances that is in the process of being completed; the situation which has just passed or is now passing. In effect, events or circumstances in the querent's past, as shown in the first four cards, created a general personal environment in which he or she was operating. This environment is now changing, either because the querent has taken steps to change it, or because some outside influence is forcing a change.

SIXTH CARD: *This is before you.* Place this card to the left of the Significator. It describes the future influence or set of circumstances the querent can expect; the change in personal environment that either should (if the querent is being advised what to do) or will (if he or she is just going with the flow) take place. The past, described by card five, is giving way to this new situation as a result of the actions the querent is taking, or goals to which he or she aspires, or any influences, internal or external, as described by the previous cards.

[Note: Cards five and six can also be used as a "time-check"; a way to determine how long a period of time the reading covers.]

This can be very helpful, since one of the questions you will be asked about the results of a reading is when all of this is actually going to happen. Your clue is in card five: if you can determine when those circumstances occurred or existed, you'll have a fairly good idea of when future events will take place as well.

To use these cards as a time-check, explain the nature of the situation described by card five, and ask the querent how long ago it occurred or existed. The events or situations described by card six will happen approximately that far in the future—and so will the general outcome of the reading as a whole.

Since card five describes something in the querent's past, it should not be difficult to identify it. However, you have to make certain that you describe it clearly enough so that the querent understands exactly what incident or set of circumstances you're talking about. Be obscure, and they may pick the wrong situation—and therefore the wrong period of time—as their answer. Only the querent can tell you how long ago these changes or events took place; if their information is inaccurate, so will be your prediction of how long they have to wait for everything to be resolved.

If you don't use these cards as a time-check, you can still get an idea of the approximate time range for the reading. Before you start the reading, specify the amount of time you want it to cover—anywhere from a few days up to 12 months. You can't force the future to resolve itself within a specified period of time! But you can ask the cards to confine their predictions to that period of time.

And, of course, there are readings in which you don't need a time-check at all. If the querent is asking about a specific event he or she expects to be involved in, then you already know when it's going to happen, and all you need to know is how it will come out.

With the first six cards on the table, your spread is now arranged in the form of a cross, with the Significator in the center, under the first card. The last four cards will be laid out to the right of this cross, starting at the lower right, and placed one above the other.

CARD SEVEN: *This is you.* This card represents the querent. In general, it places the querent in perspective in terms of the circumstances of the reading. It shows the querent's stance, or attitude toward him or herself and/or toward the situation. As a result, it also reveals how the querent is likely to behave or react in this situation.

CARD EIGHT: *This is your house.* Card eight is placed directly above card seven. It represents the querent's environment, or surroundings, in this situation; what is going on around the querent at this time. It shows the querent's effect on other people, especially those close to him or her, or closely involved in the situation, and the querent's effect on events in general.

More important, it also reveals what kind of effect those other people or events will have on the querent or on the outcome of the situation; what they're doing, how they're reacting, and/or what their intentions are in these circumstances.

CARD NINE: *This is your hopes and fears.* Place this card above Card Eight. This card reveals the querent's innermost thoughts regarding this situation. It shows how the querent feels about the people, events, and circumstances surrounding him or her at this time including the querent's feelings about self and his or her chances for success or failure.

There are two facts about this card which you need to make sure the querent understands. First, the card describes how the querent *feels;* not what has happened, is happening, or will happen. Not everyone's emotional perspective is accurate! The querent's reaction may be reasonable given the circumstances, but it could also be entirely off-base (in which case, you tell them that they can't see the forest for the trees!).

Second, whether the querent's emotional perspective is accurate or not, it will still affect the outcome. If the querent has to take action on something, for example, and is afraid to, then even if the cards predict a good possibility for success, he or she may still fail—because they can't make a move. The other cards in the reading will reveal whether or not the querent's perceptions of the situation are justified.

CARD TEN: *This is the result.* The final card in the reading is placed directly above Card Nine. It reveals what is going to happen; the culmination which will result from the influences shown by all the other cards in this reading.

As the reader, this is the card on which you focus your attention. The other cards in the reading explain how and why the querent will get to this point—and how and if this result can be encouraged or avoided. But card ten contains the answer to the querent's question: the final outcome of all of the influences described by the reading. It concludes and explains the information you've gained from all the other cards in this reading, including the card you chose as the Significator. And note here: if card ten is a Minor Arcana court card, then it does represent a person—and that person holds the outcome of this situation in his or her hands.

If the reading is obviously answering your question but the meaning of card ten is obscure in any way, it is a valid reason to repeat the reading, in order to clarify the answer. In that case, you use this card as your Significator in the repeat reading, instead of the card you initially used. Note: If you repeat the reading, put the other ten cards back in the deck (your original Significator, and cards one through nine), then reshuffle and cut the entire deck (minus your new Significator) as before.

An Example of a Celtic Spread

This reading was done for a young man in his early 30s. He put a lot of work into preparing for his chosen profession and building his business, and his social life suffered as a result.

He admits that he's always been socially inept (you have to learn to be popular, too!); he also admits that he's spent more time developing his professional skills than seeking relationships. But he's wondering now about missed opportunities. His stated question:

Has anyone ever been in love with me? Despite the fact that the question involves love and romance, the Significator chosen to represent the querent was the Knight of Wands. The choice was based on the type of person this young man is; a self-starter, ambitious, hard-working, and beginning to see some prospects of success. It is, after all, his involvement with career, and the resultant neglect of social opportunities and skills, which is the basis of this situation.

Here are the cards that came out. [Note: Cards are upright unless otherwise specified.]

FIRST CARD (This covers you): *Page of Cups, reversed.* A card from the suit of love which describes seduction and deceit.

With a court card, the first thing you want to establish is whether or not the card represents a person, and if so, who. There have been young women in this man's life, some of whom he has been very fond of, and he has had some tentative relationships which have fallen apart. There is no one, however, who meets this description: a friend or lover who deliberately deceived him.

This card, then, does not represent someone else. However, the covering card describes the basis of the situation, including the querent's attitude, which is that he has not paid serious attention to developing relationships. This card, then, represents the querent—and answers his stated question! If he's trying to convince himself that some woman from his past is desperately in love with him, he's only deceiving himself. And then the reading goes on from there.

What do you do when the first card answers the question? One very good possibility is that the stated question was not what the querent really meant to ask, or really needed to know.

This turned out to be the case. This young man feels the lack of someone to share his life. But he has trouble meeting new people, and he hasn't really been willing, yet, to put the time into looking. So he was hoping that the woman of his dreams was looking for him. The cards say it's not going to be that easy.And then they go on from there to tell him what he does have to do.

SECOND CARD (This crosses you): *Eight of Swords, reversed*; a card of sickness and injury. This card explains why, in his past, he has not had any serious relationships. Translating "sickness" to mean something that weakens you, the card refers partly to his own social ineptitude, and partly to his prior unwillingness to work at establishing a lasting relationship. The injury is the one he's done to himself, and he's paying for it with loneliness.

THIRD CARD (This crowns you): *Seven of Coins, reversed*. This card provides a good example of how suits can switch their perspective. Cards from the suit of Coins generally refer to money matters; the seven reversed indicates an uncertain or unwise expenditure. But since the question involves love, the expenditure here is most probably emotional. Yes, it costs money to go out on dates, and he has spent some on that activity. His real problem is that he needs to find someone to love, and what he's wasting is time and energy hoping it will just happen for him. As the song goes, he's looking for love in all the wrong places. And evidently, since this is the best he can expect under the circumstances, this "unwise expenditure" will continue unless he changes his ways.

FOURTH CARD (This is beneath you): *The Knight of Swords*; a treacherous and malicious enemy. Again, since no one, male or female, has ever deliberately set out to hurt him in the area of relationships, the question is: who's the real enemy here? Remember that the lack of relationships in his past has been mostly his own doing. In this situation, then, the Knight of Swords suggests that his worst enemy is himself.

FIFTH CARD (This is behind you): *The Four of Swords, reversed*; greed. So his past was one in which he was evidently expecting something to which he was not entitled. He expected love to happen to him without having to work at it. Greed indeed! We know, however, from the position of the card that this is changing. What's it changing to?

Time Check—Since we're talking about an emotional state rather than a specific event, it's difficult to establish an exact time frame. The best thing to do in this case is to allow a little leeway, by going back to the origin of the situation on which the question is based. To the querent's best recollection, then, it was about six months prior to the date of the reading that he began to realize that success in business was not all he wanted out of life; and also around that time he began wishing he had someone to share his life with. If we've identified the right set of circumstances, the changes shown in the next card should be fully established sometime within the next six months; and the final outcome predicted by the reading should be within his reach at that time as well.

SIXTH CARD (This is befroe you): *The King of Wands reversed;* describes an austere but tolerant man. Note that this card is from the same suit as the Significator, and that it appears in a future-outcome position. Court cards from the same suit as the Significator show up in readings more often than can be ascribed to coincidence.

In general, such a card definitely refers back to the querent; it shows him in a different position or set of circumstances than the original card. In this case, because it describes his new personal environment, it also describes the change in him that is beginning to happen.

So what does this card tell us? The Significator was the Knight of Wands, and this is a young man who is on his way to professional success. The King card in this position—describing something that will happen in the future—suggests that he will get there, but also indicates a definite change in his general attitude. He is changing from the self-destructive Swords behavior to a more tolerant, mature attitude. In effect, he's going to grow up emotionally. And that should have a positive effect on his future relationships.

SEVENTH CARD (This is you): *Seven of Cups;* fresh but indefinite ideas in the mind of the querent, indicating a change of attitude but no concrete plans at this time. He knows he's been going about this the wrong way and that he has to change his approach, but he's not quite sure exactly what to do. Specifically, he's beginning to realize that if he wants love, he'll have to work as hard at that as he does at his business. Now all he has to do is figure out how.

But it is a beginning. And it's also the reason that the change of attitude or personality, from the one shown in card five to the one predicted by card six, is likely to happen.

EIGHTH CARD (This is your house): *The Chariot.* The divinatory meaning which best applies here is mastery of opposing forces; and since this is Major Arcana, the victory must be as much over himself as over circumstances. He has to reconcile his business interests and his social needs; to be willing to give at least as much time and effort to a woman he might care about as he does his business concerns. But that, for this querent, is the least of it.

In order to succeed in this situation, he has to overcome his own diffidence, to make himself able to function in social settings. Since this card appears in his present environment, evidently he is beginning to take steps in this direction—and will eventually be successful at it.

CARD NINE (This is your hopes and fears): *Ace of Wands, reversed*; a card of ruin and decline. Again, based on the choice of Significator, this is a card from the querent's own suit—and it expresses his feelings about this new beginning he's making. He expects to fail.

Based on the other cards in his spread, however, he should not fail; these feelings come from his own basic insecurities. Understand that what we're dealing with here is not a selfish workaholic, but someone who is basically shy. If he's put all his effort up until now into his profession it's because that's something he knows he can do. He's not sure at all that even if he makes the effort he'll be able to find someone to love him.

CARD TEN (This is the result): *Justice*; a victory of the right. The outcome is in his own hands; he will get what he deserves. And since other cards in the reading show that he's willing to make the effort, and that victory is within his grasp, the chances are very good that what he deserves is what he wants and hopes for: he will find someone to love.

Now let's take a look at the reading as a whole. What kind of cards came up here?

Two Major Arcana (self-change and development). Three court cards, not counting the Significator, which in this reading also describe the querent, even though they're all from different suits. Swords (self-destruction) in his past; love in his heart; and justice in his future.

The one suit that appears more than any other is Swords, though these destructive influences are all in his past. But note the Justice card also carries a sword, in this case obviating the negative influence in the future. He's no longer on the self-destructive course; now he's fighting for himself instead of against himself.

There is no real ruling suit in this reading, but there is a general theme. The court cards describe the querent, plus the Major Arcana tells us that the key to this situation is the querent's own personal development. He's been going through some serious problems and personal changes, but now he's beginning to come out the other end.

So what is the answer to his question? No, he's never been loved before, nor has he ever really been in love. In fact, he's expecting something to which the person he was is simply not entitled (greed card). But that is all in his past, because the person he was is changing.

The King of Wands especially in this reading is a very positive sign. Maturity and experience result in abilities and attitudes that youth lacks. He's still shy and unsure of himself (Card Nine), but not in the same way or to the same extent as when he was younger. And as he matures—as he develops his own inner confidence—he will be able to improve his ability to initiate and participate in relationships as well.

So the answer—to his unspoken question—is yes. He will be able to find the love he's looking for, and in the foreseeable future.

I know you want to know what happened next.

The reading was done about three months before it was written into this book. That puts us about halfway through the time-frame suggested by card five. If both the reading and the time-check are accurate, the querent should be making some progress toward his goal. So where is he now?

Well, he hasn't become a social butterfly in that short time! But he has made the effort to get involved in purely social activities. As a result, he's met several young women he finds compatible, and one in particular who in his eyes stands out from the crowd. There are no wedding bells planned as yet. On the other hand, he's happy enough in his current situation that he doesn't feel the need for another reading on this same question. And that's the best sign of all!

As you can see, even a reading using only ten cards can tell you a lot about the person's circumstances and expectations. Now let's see what we can get from a spread that uses even fewer cards.

A Five-Card Spread

This is an even simpler spread that works very well for minor inquiries. It uses only the twenty-two cards of the Major Arcana; Minor Arcana cards are removed from the deck before shuffling.

It's generally not necessary to use a Significator, since the reading as a whole refers directly to the querent. You would need a Significator only if the question is being asked for or about someone else. In that case, it is the only card you'll take from the Minor Arcana.

Preparation of the deck is also simpler. With the Minor Arcana cards removed from the deck, the cards are shuffled by the reader. They do not have to be cut, nor does the querent have to handle the cards. The querent's input will be in the selection of the cards used for the spread.

If you use a Significator, place it in the center of the table above where you will lay out your cards; none of the cards in this spread will cover the Significator. Lay out the five cards of the spread in a single horizontal line from right to left; the rightmost card is Card One (See Figure Two).

When the cards are shuffled, the querent is asked to pick a number from one to twenty-two. If the querent chooses ten, for example, the reader counts down through the cards and takes out the tenth card. This is laid on the table as Card One.

Then the cards are shuffled again, and the querent is asked for another number (which, obviously, must be twenty-one or less). The second card is chosen by the same process as the first. Continue this process, shuffling the deck each time and asking for a different number each time. You may shuffle for these subsequent picks either once, twice, or three times, as long as you do it the same for each of the four remaining cards.

In this spread each of the five cards has its own name, and its own effect on the interpretation of the reading. They are read as follows:

CARD ONE: *Affirmation*. This is what is going to happen. Note: this is not an answer to the question, as happened in our first reading. The cards are simply telling you that no matter what you asked, or what you hope for, this is what you're going to get.

CARD TWO: *Negation*. This is what can or will prevent it from happening.

CARD THREE: *Discussion or Explanation*. This is why you're in this situation.

CARD FOUR: *Solution*. This is what you can do about it, to either encourage or change it.

CARD FIVE: *Determination, or Synthesis*. Depending on what steps you take, this is what will happen—or what you can make happen—instead.

This spread does not have an outcome, or answer, card as does the Celtic spread. The five cards as a unit provide an answer to your question.

An Example of a Five-Card Spread

Here's a sample reading, utilizing this method. For this reading, the querent did not ask a question; he simply chose five different numbers, not in any particular order. The result (and interpretation) of the reading was as follows:

CARD ONE (Affirmation): *The Falling Tower*. You are heading for absolute and total destruction of all your plans and dreams.

CARD TWO (Negation): *The Fool*. You can avoid this disaster if you stop acting like a jerk.

CARD THREE (Discussion): *The Devil*. What is the foolish thing you're doing? You are putting your hopes for your destiny into the power of a force that cares nothing at all for you.

CARD FOUR (Solution): *The High Priest*. What should you do? Stop hoping that this other force will solve your problems and take your destiny into your own hands.

CARD FIVE (Determination): *The World*. The result, if you get your act together, will be absolute attainment and success.

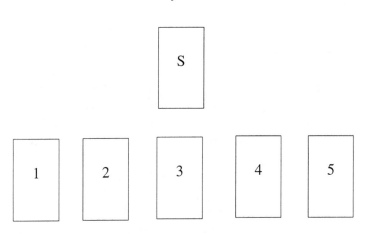

Figure Two: Five-Card Spread

Well that's good enough advice in a variety of situations. The question is, what does it mean in terms of this querent?

Before this reading can make any sense to you, you have to understand what happened. The friend I read for did not ask a definite question; however, he also couldn't think of five random numbers. So he used the numbers that he plays every week in the state lottery to select the cards for this reading. Three of the numbers he normally plays were higher than twenty-two, so he added the two digits together. He also normally plays a series of six numbers, but two of them added to the same single-digit number, and that gave him five numbers.

This particular reading illustrates a couple of interesting facts about the way the Tarot works. Fact One: As we saw in the Celtic reading, no matter what question you ask aloud, the cards will answer the one you're really thinking about. In this case, no question was stated aloud, but since the querent used his lottery numbers, obviously somewhere in his mind was the question of whether or not he was ever going to win.

Fact Two: If you ask a stupid question, you're going to get an uppity answer. The Tarot cards—at least, the ones in my deck!—really resent being bothered with questions about the possibility of winning at games of chance.

So here's what the reading really means, in terms of this querent and his unspoken/unconscious question:

If you keep putting your money on the lottery, you're going to keep losing it. Instead of pinning your hopes for wealth on the lottery, if you want to have lots of money, stop wishing for it and start working for it.

Short, sweet, and to the point, and, because the spread utilizes only the Major Arcana, brutally honest. The Tarot doesn't pull a single punch!

The next spread uses seven cards, but it's actually the simplest of all.

A Seven-Card Spread

As you've seen, very often the Tarot provides an explanation, rather than a straightforward answer. You're told not only what can happen but why, and what will change it and how, plus a wealth of other comments and insights into both the situation and the personal attributes of the querent.

Not all questions require that kind of detail. Sometimes you just want a quick and simple answer. This last spread can be interpreted in detail if you choose, or simply used to answer yes or no. Note: This spread cannot be used for a general reading; you must ask a definite question, and it must be phrased so that it can be answered yes or no.

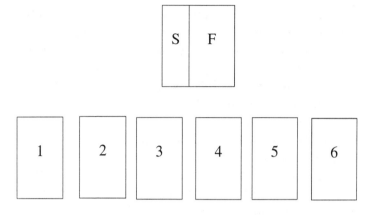

Figure Three: Seven-Card Spread

Once the deck has been shuffled and cut, lay out the first seven cards into your spread from right to left (see Figure Three). If you are going to interpret the cards individually, the first three cards represent the past, or the events leading up to this situation. The last three cards reveal the future, or how the situation will conclude. The center card is called the Focus Card; it will give you the most information about the situation. The focus card should be placed on top of the Significator when it is dealt out.

Note: If you are going to interpret the cards individually, the focus card can also serve as a Significator chosen by the Tarot; i.e., rather than choosing a Significator up front, you interpret the center card as the reason for the spread's answer to your question.

Here's how it works. The querent asks his or her question, and the cards are shuffled and cut for the reading. The cards are laid out in order from right to left (the focus card will be the fourth card placed into the spread). Any cards which appear upright in the spread mean yes; reversed cards mean no. The first three and last three cards are valued at one point each; the focus card is worth two points. A simple bit of arithmetic does the rest; add up the yes and no points and you have your answer.

This spread also provides a quick and easy way to determine whether or not the cards will answer a particular question for the querent. If the results come out even, then the querent must make his or her own decision on this matter without any help from the Tarot.

An Example of a Seven-Card Spread

Here's a sample reading. This question was asked by a mother about her daughter. The daughter, a young woman in her early twenties, was scheduled for surgery in less than two weeks; the mother wanted to know if she would come through it all right.

Of the seven cards in the spread, four of them, including the focus card, were reversed; three were upright. That made five negative points and three positive—a definite no.

With an answer like that, and especially considering the seriousness of the situation, we naturally wanted to know what was going on. The type of surgery the daughter was facing was not that dangerous a procedure, and the young woman herself was basically in good health, except for this one problem. Why the dire warning? Here's what the Tarot had to say about it.

The Significator chosen was the Page of Wands, since "saucy and mischievous" certainly describes this young woman's character. These were the cards dealt into the spread:

CARD ONE (Past Influences): *Six of Swords, upright:* a journey of uncertain destination. Obviously this refers to the surgery itself, since the querent didn't know how it was going to work out. But it could have another meaning in this context:

CARD TWO: *The Falling Tower, reversed:* calamities of a lesser importance in kind. This could refer to the operation itself: the surgery was not supposed to be that serious, and—except for the fact that any surgery is a risk—not life-threatening. But what if the meaning of this card is that the daughter's illness was not serious enough to require surgery in the first place?

CARD THREE: *Justice, reversed.* Abuse of justice; bigotry. That possibility would seem to be confirmed by this card. The family involved here are immigrants. They've done well in this country, and they can afford medical treatment, but they are not entirely knowledge-able about how the system works. A smooth-talking doctor with priorities of his own could talk them into something that they don't need.

CARD FOUR (Focus Card): *Two of Wands, reversed;* a surprise of some kind; some unexpected factor enter-ing into the situation. And note that here, too, the focus card is from the same suit as the Significator. The two of Wands is generally not a fortunate card, and the sur-prise may be either pleasant or unpleasant (or, as it turned out in this case, both). But obviously, something new is going to affect this situation—and, since it is from her suit, it has to do specifically with the daughter.

CARD FIVE (Future Results): Death, upright. Death, failure. As far as the Tarot is concerned, if this young woman has the surgery, she's running a mortal risk. She may not die on the table, but the surgery is bound to cause more problems than it solves.

CARD SIX: *Ten of Wands, upright.* A gamble for high stakes. The meaning here is clear. What this young woman is gambling with is her life. And the question at this point is whether or not she should have this surgery at all.

CARD SEVEN: *Four of Cups, reversed.* New relationships; an unforeseen event. A confirmation of the focus card; something is going to change. In this case, however, it will change because of new people, and potentially friendly ones, given the suit, that either the querent or her daughter are soon to meet.

This reading illustrates just how definitely a Tarot reading can change your future.

The first question I asked after getting these results was how many doctors they had seen before scheduling this surgery. The answer was only this one. Over the next week, however, they consulted three more—and not one of them recommended surgery for the daughter's medical problem. The problem was real, but all three "second opinions" prescribed a course of medication for her condition. With the proper medication, it took a little more than three weeks for her condition to clear up entirely, and she never had the totally unnecessary surgery.

And I hardly need add that this was one of the most satisfying readings I'd done in a long while. Results like this are why you take the time and trouble to learn to read the Tarot cards.

Conclusion

So where does all this leave you? You start with a peculiar-looking deck of seventy-eight cards and a book that lists pages of interpretations for each one of them. You know that this deck holds within it the answers to your important questions. How do you make it render up those answers to you?

In order to do an accurate reading, you have to know the meanings of the cards, but unless you have total recall, simply memorizing all that information is an impossible task. And even with a photographic memory, it's a pretty pointless one. The lists of words and phrases given as divinatory interpretations are meaningless in and of themselves. You have to use them in a reading to understand how they apply to real-life situations. Which makes it a kind of Catch-22: in order to use them you have to know them, but in order to know them you have to use them.

In addition, for both the Major and Minor Arcana, I told you that not all of the definitions given for any one card apply at the same time. You not only have to know all the definitions, you have to know how to pick the one that makes sense in the context of the reading.

Determining the exact interpretation of any card in a reading is simply a matter of experience. You learn, over time, what each of the listed interpretations actually mean as they apply to real situations. And you also learn how to determine what the most logical interpretation is in a specific reading.

However, that kind of explanation does you little good. This is a beginner's book after all!—it is no help to be told, as you have been told throughout this book, that "With experience you'll be able to..." So before we close, let's talk about how you get that experience.

You'll find that most people are intrigued by the idea of having their cards read. And many of them are also willing to be patient with a neophyte reader. If you don't try to set yourself up as an expert diviner from the beginning, you can use input and feedback from your first consultants to teach you how to understand the cards.

So, when you start doing readings, just tell people that you're a beginner. They'll wait while you look up the meanings of the cards. And they'll tell you how those interpretations apply to their questions. If you're willing to stumble at first, if you're willing to admit that you're not infallible even once you become more expert, you can learn to understand what the Tarot is trying to tell you. Work *with* the querent, learn from other people's lives and experiences as well as your own, and I guarantee you that before you know it, you'll be making the right associations on your own. It's as simple as that.

There are two other points to keep in mind that will help you figure out what you're seeing in a spread. First, not every situation—in fact, very few of them at all—will be world-shaking. It is a fact that sometimes, as you saw in the third sample reading, the information you uncover can be a matter of life and death. But just as often, as you saw in the second reading, it will not involve a life-changing experience even for the querent. Don't "reach" for extraordinary explanations of what you see in the cards. You're reading for ordinary people after all. Their problems and questions are important, never doubt it, ; but the answers they need, and will get from the cards, are not likely to be mystical revelations of enormous import. Expect the ordinary, not the unusual. Or, as the old medical saw goes: When you hear hoofbeats, think horses, not zebras.

The second point is this: very often, and especially when you're working with a spread that focuses on the Major Arcana, interpreting the Tarot cards can be like interpreting your dreams. You won't get the messages spelled out in plain English; you get images, symbolism, and hints which you then have to relate to the people involved and to the question that was asked. In short, you have to think about the message you're getting to understand what it means, and how it applies to your life.

But again, the more that you practice reading the cards, the clearer these images will become. And eventually you will reach the point where you know, just by looking at a completed spread, what the answer is. And the only reason you'll need to interpret each individual card is to get the details.

The hard part is getting started. It's not easy to learn to read the Tarot cards, but it can be done. Don't get discouraged if it takes you a while to develop the skills you need; it's not because you haven't got the ability, it's because it's a difficult and complex skill!

Whether you use the cards for meditation only, or for getting answers to your own questions, or to read for others, it's worth the time and work you'll put into it. Enjoy the trip. When you arrive, you'll find that the Tarot can be your best and most faithful Guide.

Conclusion

YOUR FUTURE IN YOUR CARDS

Despite the mass of information you've been given in this text, this is not by any means a conclusion to your study of the Tarot; it is only a beginning.

One flaw that all explanations of the Tarot have in common is that each system is, perforce, self-contained. Even those which, like this text, advise you to examine other sources as well can only take you just so far. There may be an infinite number of interpretations of the cards, but there is, after all, only a finite number of cards to interpret. And once each text has detailed its own system for understanding and using the Tarot, there is no place else for it to go.

But there's no limit to how far you can go, because the Tarot itself can take you anywhere you choose.

My best advice for growing with the Tarot is this. Once you've learned the basics, as outlined here, investigate as many different systems as you can get your hands on (or afford!). Read other books on the subject; examine a number of decks. You may have to take some wrong turns along your path; that is, wrong for you. Until you've seen at least some variety in both interpretations and deck designs, however, you won't be able to decide what works best for you.

There are a lot of options available for you to explore. Tarot texts range from the sketchy and incomplete versions you find in occult compendiums to highly detailed (and occasionally incomprehensibly mystical) volumes explaining every possible aspect and use of the cards. Tarot deck designs range from simple, straightforward depictions, some of them professionally drawn and some delightfully primitive, to extremely complex works of art, covered with magical symbols which sometimes heighten and sometimes obscure the basic meaning of the allegory on each card.

Among all the systems you examine, there will be some you feel more than reward you for your efforts, and some which you consider a complete waste of your time. But each deck, no matter how it's drawn, and each text, no matter how well or poorly written, has something to offer the serious scholar. Don't be impatient with other peoples' view of the Tarot, even those that seem to wander far afield, and even when your instincts tell you that a given explanation must be wrong. (In fact, it's when you start getting a feeling that someone is right or wrong that you know you're finally beginning to understand the Tarot and to arrive at your own unique interpretations of the cards.)

Most especially, don't be impatient with those writers whose overall perspective on the Tarot is very different from your own. You need them most of all. *Because* their needs are so different and their personal goals so unrelated to what you would seek, they open a window that you would not find on your own. Use them to discover how many different visions the Tarot makes possible. This ancient book of wisdom can be made to fit any version of reality; and the more versions of reality you see, the more likely it is that you will be able to find your own truth someday.

It is a fact that there are a few writers on the Tarot who are dogmatic, from those who claim to have the only valid interpretation of the cards to those who "correct" the meaning of the cards to fit a single, narrow vision. In every generation, there have been interpreters who had a political point to make, and so explained the Tarot either to support one or another of their century's philosophies or to refute them.

Although such writers have always been with us, they are also very much in the minority. Most of the variant explanations you'll find are simply written by interpreters who have found in the Tarot a voice for their visions, and are trying to share it with you. You'll find some of these interpretations illuminating, and some confusing, some fascinating and some ridiculous. Some may disturb or perhaps anger you, even if they don't claim superior insight; but even if a given vision of the Tarot is not one you can accept, it is still a valid vision. It is more than worth your time to see the many roads down which the Tarot can take you.

One thing is certain: no matter how different one interpretation may be from another, there is ultimately no right or wrong explanation of the cards. They're ALL right—and they may all be wrong, depending on your focus.

The reason everyone reacts differently to the Tarot is simple: every person is different. Your individual personality and set of life's experiences as well as spiritual needs give you a unique perspective on how you respond to what you see. In the Major Arcana especially, each picture contains such a richness and variety of symbolism that very few people can take it all in at once. So we each focus on some aspects to the exclusion of others. And sometimes that means that you can overlook something important, or overemphasize something minor.

Whatever the author's perspective, any text on the Tarot can only point out what you may miss without instruction; what you may overlook because it doesn't connect with your personal experience and needs. Any writer on the Tarot can only give you his or her own personal understanding of the meaning of the cards. But there is no complete and definitive guide to the Tarot, because there is no single, absolute definition of the cards.

The link to tie it all together, the final determination of the true meaning of the Tarot, is you.

The Tarot is a key—and where there's a key, there's a door. And somewhere on the other side of this particular door you will find the answers to all your questions, simple and complex, secular and religious, spiritual and mundane. Let those who have gone before you show you what doors the Tarot has opened for them. Gather as much information as you can; explore as many other viewpoints as you can. Learn to take from each what you need to heighten your own understanding of the Tarot.

And then go on your own path from there. Let the Tarot take you where it will; let it help you create your own vision of what is true and what is real. And if that vision continually changes each time you pick up your cards, that's only because you are also changing as you grow and as you learn. Don't let it confuse you. Take it as a sign that you're growing closer to the answers you need.

One day, if you're lucky, it will all come together, and you'll see the path that you need to recreate yourself and your understanding of the universe. When that happens, you will finally be a master of the Tarot.

Divining with the Tarot

This book is divided into two sections; let's divide the conclusion the same way.

It should be clear by this point that my emphasis is on using the Tarot for meditation, and for spiritual self-development. But if all you want is a simple fortune-telling method, that's fine, too. I certainly use my deck for divination, and I've done so for years. The Tarot is, after all, a superb divination tool, and it would be foolish to overlook or belittle that use of the cards.

Assuming that you will use your cards for divination, then there is one very important message I want to leave you with. I mentioned it earlier, but I want to stress it now. Because if you don't remember this—and if you don't make sure the people you read for are aware of this—it can make others doubt your abilities, and worse, it could make you doubt yourself.

There is no absolute destiny: there is only cause and effect. Sometimes the process is clear. If you mix blue and yellow, you're going to get green. If you add two and two you're going to get four. Cause and effect.

Most of life's situations are so complex that it's difficult if not impossible to determine what effect your actions will cause. And those are the situations for which you need a means of prophecy; a way to see clearly what will happen.

The point to remember is that if you change the cause, you change the effect. And that means that if a future result you predicted changes, it doesn't necessarily mean the prophecy was wrong.

If I tell you that mixing blue with yellow will give you green, and green is something you cannot endure for whatever reason, you can mix blue with red instead and get purple. You've changed the effect—but you haven't changed the accuracy of my prophecy. Because if you had mixed blue with yellow, you would have gotten green. YOU decided not to cause the green; you took steps to replace one result with another. All I did was tell you what would have happened had you continued, all unknowing, on the course you originally meant to take. If you use your cards for fortunetelling, you will see this effect again and again. You will predict—accurately!—what lies in someone's immediate future. Then, because that individual was forewarned, they will be able to take steps to change their future. If they indeed change their future, it doesn't mean you were wrong. It means you served your purpose. You fulfilled the function of a true prophet.

A familiar story which illustrates this is that of the prophet Jonah.

According to Jewish teachings, Jonah was ordered by God to go to Nineveh and warn the people there that the city would be destroyed because of their sin. Jonah did not want to go. (This is why he ran away, and how he wound up in the belly of a whale. Read the original story for these details; we don't need them here.) He didn't want to go because he knew what would happen, because it had happened to him before, and he didn't want it to happen again.

What did happen? After his slap on the wrist from God, Jonah grudgingly trekked over to Nineveh, marched into the city, and announced that the entire population and everything they possessed would be destroyed by God because they were sinners.

Well, both the king and the people of Nineveh had had some experience with such prophecies in the past, and they believed every word. So they put on sackcloth and ashes and declared a period of fast during which they repented their sins.

And God, seeing that their repentance was genuine, withdrew the judgment previously passed against Nineveh and did not destroy the city after all.

Now this was exactly what Jonah knew would happen, and exactly why he didn't want to go in the first place. It wasn't that he wanted to see the people of Nineveh destroyed; the story makes it clear that he didn't care about them one way or the other. But he was, after all, a genuine prophet; a man who actually spoke to God. And he felt that when these genuine prophecies didn't come true as stated, it made him look like a fraud or, worse, like a fool.

Jonah missed the point. Don't you miss it, too. The point is that even divinely decreed decisions about your future are not immutable. If you take steps to change your actions, even God will change the decree. How much simpler, then, must it be to change relatively minor events for which you, and not God, are the deciding factor?

The future is not predetermined; you can control what direction your life will take—*if you have accurate information on which to base your decision.*

With the Tarot, you have it within your power to gather the information you need, both for yourself and for others.

The reason for prophecy is not to show off how accurate the prophet is. It's to give the person for whom the prophecy was made an opportunity to see what effect they're causing. Change the cause and you change the effect.

So be aware that just the fact that you tell someone their possible future can alter that future. As the Tarot reader, don't worry, as Jonah did, about looking like a fool because your prophecy will be changed. And most important, you must not begin to doubt your own gift of prophecy, simply because the person for whom you prophesied was able to take the information you gave them and use it to change their destiny. Just remember that it was your (accurate!) information that enabled someone to get themselves out of a bad situation that they wouldn't have even seen coming if not for you.

So here are the rules for telling fortunes. First: call it as you see it. Never downplay what you see in the cards, never hedge your explanations. If what you see is disaster, don't predict sweetness and light just to make the person feel better. Explain clearly whatever you see coming, and, as much as you can, why. The querent needs to know what you can tell them, important or minor, good or bad. They need the facts, so they can make a viable decision.

Second: if, as a result of your reading, the effect you predicted doesn't happen, don't begin to doubt

your abilities—and certainly don't feel bad when someone comes back and tells you that they were able to
make a change. If your prediction enables someone to
avoid a disaster, or even just to make things a little bit
better than they might have been, that's certainly no
reason to feel you failed!

Yes; tell every person for whom you read that they
can use this information to change their future if they
choose. That's part of the information they need. But if
the querent does in fact change his or her future, it simply means you've been of greater help to them than in
any reading you do that comes out exactly as predicted.
You haven't erred. You've served your purpose.

Be true to yourself, and be truthful to those for
whom you read. You have in your hands a tool that you
can use to change your own life, or that you can use to
enable others to make changes in their lives as well.

One Final Note

The Tarot offers a richness of experience and insight to
anyone willing to approach it with an open mind; not
only in the variety of paths it opens to the Seeker, but also
in the irony and even humor in many of the cards. The
originators of the Tarot were wise; they saw the wacki-
ness in the human condition as well as its potential.

The Tarot is unquestionably a serious and important tool for both meditation and divination, but don't
cheat yourself by missing the fact that, just like the
human condition it pictures, it can simply be fun, too.

Learn from your cards, and grow with them, but
don't forget to enjoy them as well. And may you find
what you are seeking.

On the following pages you will find listed, with their current prices, some of the books now available on related subjects. Your book dealer stocks most of these and will stock new titles in the Llewellyn series as they become available. We urge your patronage.

TO GET A FREE CATALOG

To obtain our full catalog, you are invited to write (see address below) for our bi-monthly news magazine/catalog, *Llewellyn's New Worlds of Mind and Spirit*. A sample copy is free, and it will continue coming to you at no cost as long as you are an active mail customer. Or you may subscribe for just $10 in the United States and Canada ($20 overseas, first class mail). Many bookstores also have *New Worlds* available to their customers. Ask for it.

TO ORDER BOOKS AND TAPES

If your book store does not carry the titles described on the following pages, you may order them directly from Llewellyn by sending the full price in U.S. funds, plus postage and handling (see below).

Credit card orders: VISA, MasterCard, American Express are accepted. Call toll-free within the USA and Canada at 1-800-THE-MOON.

Special Group Discount: Because there is a great deal of interest in group discussion and study of the subject matter of this book, we offer a 20% quantity discount to group leaders or agents. Our Special Quantity Price for a minimum order of five copies of *Tarot for Beginners* is $51.80 cash-with-order. Include postage and handling charges noted below.

Postage and Handling: Include $4 postage and handling for orders $15 and under; $5 for orders *over* $15. There are no postage and handling charges for orders over $100. Postage and handling rates are subject to change. We ship UPS whenever possible within the continental United States; delivery is guaranteed. Please provide your street address as UPS does not deliver to P.O. boxes. Orders shipped to Alaska, Hawaii, Canada, Mexico and Puerto Rico will be sent via first class mail. Allow 4-6 weeks for delivery. **International orders:** Airmail – add retail price of each book and $5 for each non-book item (audiotapes, etc.); Surface mail – add $1 per item.

Minnesota residents add 7% sales tax.

Mail orders to:
Llewellyn Worldwide
P.O. Box 64383-K-363, St. Paul, MN 55164-0383, U.S.A.

For customer service, call (612) 291-1970.

THE WITCHES TAROT
The Witches Qabala, Book II
by Ellen Cannon Reed

In this book Ellen Cannon Reed has further defined the complex, inner workings of the Qabalistic Tree of Life. She brings together the Major and Minor Arcana cards with the Tree of Life to provide readers with a unique insight on the meaning of the Paths on the Tree. Included is a complete section on divination with the Tarot cards, with several layout patterns and explanations clearly presented.

THE PRINCESS OF SWORDS

The Major Arcana cards are also keys to Pathworking astral journeys through the Tree of Life. Reed explains Pathworking and gives several examples. An appendix gives a list of correspondences for each of the Paths including the associated Tarot card, Hebrew letter, colors, astrological attribution, animal, gem, and suggested meditation. This book is a valuable addition to the literature of the Tarot and the Qabala.

0–87542–668–9, 320 pgs., 5¼x 8, illus., softcover   **$9.95**

THE WITCHES TAROT DECK
by Ellen Cannon Reed and Martin Cannon

Author Ellen Cannon Reed has created the first Tarot deck specifically for Pagans and Wiccans. Reed, herself a Wiccan High Priestess, developed The Witches Tarot as a way to teach the truths of the Hebrew Kabbalah from a clear and distinctly Pagan point of view. Changes include a Horned One in place of the traditional Devil, a High Priest in place of the old Hierophant, and a Seeker in place of the Hermit. Comes complete with an instruction booklet that tells you what the cards mean and explains how to use the "Celtic Cross" and "Four Seasons" layouts. The gorgeous, detailed paintings by Martin Cannon make this a true combination of new beauty and ancient symbolism. Even many non-pagans have reported excellent results with the cards and appreciate their colorful and timeless beauty.

0–87542–669–7, Boxed set:
78 full-color cards with booklet   **$17.95**

THE HEALING EARTH TAROT KIT
A Journey in Self-Discovery, Empowerment & Planetary Healing
Jyoti and David McKie

The Healing Earth Tarot Kit offers a fresh visual way to access intuitive guidance. The beautifully illustrated pack of 105 cards includes new images, suites and spreads to deal with contemporary questions and conditions, and it revitalizes those parts of the traditional tarot most relevant to today. *The Healing Earth Tarot* draws together teachings from many ancestors and many lands (including Aboriginal, African, Celtic and Native American) to reveal how our health and the earth's health interweave into the same web of power. Used with the accompanying book, which explains in simple terms how to consult and interpret the images, the cards may be drawn individually for daily guidance or laid out in appropriate spreads. Their clarity and beauty enable you to access your own inner knowing and ask for help with any aspect of your life. Each unique image has a message designed to empower you to make both everyday and momentous life decisions.

Most of the major arcana cards are presented in a new light, with several of their names altered to emphasize concern for higher awareness in ourselves. The Hermit, for example, become The Wise Old Woman and reinstates the feminine wisdom hidden deep within ourselves. The Magician has become The Shaman in the ancient tradition of wisdom and healing.

A tarot now emerges which expresses the balance of male and female, the rehonoring of our elders, and the bridge between ancient and modern ... one which can help us integrate our sensitivity, in terms of psychic and spiritual depths, by the power of the heart ... a tarot which reflects our earth community and its diversity and which points the way to healing the earth through healing the self.

BOOK: 5¼ x 8, 288 pp., softbound • illus • index
DECK: 105 cards
ISBN: 1-56718-454-5   **$34.95**

THE TAROT OF THE ORISHAS
Created by Zolrak
Illustrated by Durkon

The Deck
This remarkable new deck employs, for the first time ever, the powerful energies of Brazilian Candomble. Candomble is the living, spiritist religion that originated with the Yoruba people of west-central Africa and is similar to Santeria in its worship of the Orixás, or Orishás. Orishás are "saints," or more accurately, "Supernatural Beings"—such as "Eleggua," "Xango" ("Chango") and "Yemanya"—archetypes of sacred, powerful, and pure energy.

"The Tarot of the Orishas" consists of of 77 breathtaking, full-color cards and is based on numerology, astrology and other branches of metaphysics. Twenty-five cards represent the Orishás, and can be compared with the major arcana of the traditional Tarot. The remaining 52 cards (or "minor arcana") are divided into four groups of 13 cards each, representing the four elements.
1-56718-843-5, 77 full-color cards with instruction booklet in English & Spanish $19.95

The Kit
"The Tarot of the Orishas" Kit comes complete with the deck and book that delves into the origins and meanings of each card and ways to use the cards
1-56718-842-7, Book: In English & Spanish, 384 pgs, 6 x 9, illus., softcover; Card Deck: 77 full-color cards $29.95

Book Only:
1-56718-844-3, 384 pgs, 6 x 9, illus., softcover $12.95

THE NEW GOLDEN DAWN RITUAL TAROT DECK
by Sandra Tabatha Cicero

The original Tarot deck of the Hermetic Order of the Golden Dawn has been copied and interpreted many times. While each deck has its own special flair, The New Golden Dawn Ritual Tarot Deck may well be the most important new Tarot deck for the 1990s and beyond.

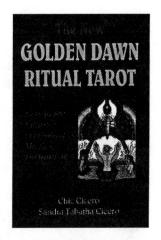

From its inception 100 years ago, the Golden Dawn continues to be the authority on the initiatory and meditative teachings of the Tarot. The Golden Dawn used certain cards in their initiation rituals. Now, for the first time ever, a deck incorporates not only the traditional Tarot images but also all of the temple symbolism needed for use in the Golden Dawn rituals. This is the first deck that is perfect both for divination and for ritual work. Meditation on the Major Arcana cards can lead to a lightning flash of enlightenment and spiritual understanding in the Western magickal tradition. The New Golden Dawn Ritual Tarot Deck was encouraged by the late Israel Regardie, and it is for anyone who wants a reliable Tarot deck that follows the Western magickal tradition.

0–87542–138–5, boxed set: 79-card deck with booklet $19.95

THE NEW GOLDEN DAWN RITUAL TAROT
Keys to the Rituals, Symbolism, Magic & Divination
by Chic Cicero & Sandra Tabatha Cicero

This is the indispensable companion to Llewellyn's New Golden Dawn Ritual Tarot Deck. It provides a card-by-card analysis of the deck's intricate symbolism, an introduction to the Qabalah, and a section on the use of the deck for practical rituals, meditations and divination procedures. The Tarot newcomer as well as the advanced magician will benefit from this groundbreaking work**0–87542–136–8, 256 pgs., 6 x 9, illus. $14.95**

LEGEND
The Arthurian Tarot
Anna-Marie Ferguson

Gallery artist and writer Anna-Marie Ferguson has paired the ancient divinatory system of the tarot with the Arthurian myth to create *Legend: The Arthurian Tarot*. The exquisitely beautiful watercolor paintings of this tarot deck illustrate characters, places and tales from the legends that blend traditional tarot symbolism with the Pagan and Christian symbolism that are equally significant elements of this myth.

Each card represents the Arthurian counterpart to tarot's traditional figures, such as Merlin as the Magician, Morgan le Fay as the Moon, Mordred as the King of Swords and Arthur as the Emperor. Accompanying the deck is a decorative layout sheet in the format of the Celtic Cross to inspire and guide your readings, as well as the book *Keeper of Words*, which lists the divinatory meanings of the cards, the cards' symbolism and the telling of the legend associated with each card.

The natural pairing of the tarot with Arthurian legend has been made before, but never with this much care, completeness and consummate artistry. This visionary tarot encompasses all the complex situations life has to offer—trials, challenges and rewards—to help you cultivate a close awareness of your past, present and future through the richness of the Arthurian legend ... a legend which continues to court the imagination and speak to the souls of people everywhere.

Complete Kit
1-56718-267-4, Book: 6 x 9, 272 pgs., illus., softcover
Deck: 78 full-color cards, Layout Sheet: 18" x 24", four-color

$34.95